KIM

KIM MORTON
with
BEATRICE ATCHESON

Causeway PRESS

Kim
© 1996 Kim Morton & Beatrice Atcheson

ISBN 1 898787 60 3

Published by

Causeway Press
9 Ebrington Terrace,
Londonderry.

Foreword

What a happiness and honour it is to write this foreword for "KIM".

I recall, as if it were yesterday, visiting the Rodgers home at Taughmonagh, Belfast, and meeting for the first time Kim, who had just started school, amid the laughter and love of her parents, and her brothers and sisters. That day Kim was jumping around and over the sofa as no-one else could!

I recall the day, some years later, when she got her special electric car and her school friends had to stand well clear as she came flying down the footpath!

The years went by, and I recall so vividly being at Kim's wedding with the lovely bride able to walk down the aisle, because of the work of those skilled in the art of prosthesis.

What a wonderful mother Kim has been over the years with three fine sons, Allan Russell and Marc.

Today Kim is centre-stage because of her valiant fight for hundreds of people in Britain who, like herself are victims of Thalidomide.

This is a story of joys and sorrows, of set-backs and achievements, and of Kim, triumphant and radiant through it all.

We are proud to read her story. For in love's service only wounded soldiers can serve. I am so glad that you are about to meet Kim through this book.

Kenneth D. Harvey

A Gift From Above

On the day my youngest sister was born, we wondered why the sun shone,
For it seemed to be the darkest day and no-one knew just what to say.
My father cried for his newborn child, would we ever again see him smile?
For one thing we all knew this baby, was loved and wanted, so why was Daddy
going crazy?

Finally after days of not knowing, baby sister came home,
And when we saw her tiny hands, at last we children could understand
Our baby sister we had waited for, lay there gurgling on the floor.

We gathered round to see our sister, all of us had sorely missed her,
She was home at last but we didn't know, fate had dealt us a terrible blow.
What had happened to her? My mother cried, what is this thing Thalidomide?

As time passed by and summer was gone, we knew why the sun had shone,.
Our baby sister was such a cutie, everyone talked of her beauty
Her determination to walk and be strong, she acted as if there was nothing
wrong.

My parents spurred on by such strong will, taught her everything, until
She walked all on her own one day, at last the sun had come to stay.
From that day on she conquered all, and with her 'limbs' she now stood tall.

She attended the same school as the rest of us, and hardly even caused a fuss
For no one who met her could fail to see how she lived life so naturally.
Her attitude made us all so proud, and she certainly stood out in a crowd.

But not because of her handicap, Oh no! our sister always stole the show
Her beauty went deeper than the skin, it shone so brightly from within
And everyone who met her would say, that she really made their day.
Her joy for life and sense of fun, touched the hearts of everyone.

~ Beatrice Atcheson 1986

Dedication

This book is dedicated to my family.

To my mother, for her love, understanding and unfaltering reassurance throughout every stage of my life. To my father, whose determination and dedication instilled in me a strong will to overcome my disability, to my brothers and sisters, who without exception have enriched my life with many wonderful childhood memories, and whose love, inspiration, strength and guidance is always there when I need it. To Eddie my husband, soul-mate and best friend, who supports me always. To my children, Allan, Russell and Marc who fill my life with laughter and an abundance of love. I consider myself to be extremely fortunate to have been born into such a loving family.

Kim Morton

Contents

CHAPTER ONE

Ten days to Number Ten

For the first time in my life, I really appreciated the wheelchair beneath me. I couldn't possibly have stood outside 10 Downing Street on that miserable, cold, wet day in March.

I hadn't eaten in 10 days, and the hunger was beginning to affect my body. My vision blurred as cameras snapped all around me. Reporters called my name over and over,

"Kim, over here! how are you bearing up? are you going to give up your hunger-strike?"

All around voices called out and everyone and everything seemed surreal to me. My head felt like cotton wool, my body was weak from the ordeal I had put it through. I was exhausted from the punishing schedule of interviews on television and radio. Answering reporters unending questions left my head spinning, but I had to hold out, I was finally here. The purpose of the hunger strike was to draw the public's attention to the Thalidomide Action Group's campaign to persuade Guinness to set up provision for a fund for the victims of Thalidomide. There in front of me was all the national media coverage I could wish for. I couldn't fail now, right in front of 10 Downing Street, I had to keep going!

Beside me stood Peter Robinson, my local MP. Behind me stood Eddie my husband, worry etched on his face, publicly supporting me, but privately pleading with me to eat before I became really ill. Heather Bird and Freddie Astbury sat alongside me also in wheelchairs, each one of us weak with hunger and weary from all the media attention. But we were driven on by a force none of us could quite put into words, but years of frustration and a felling of injustice gave us the strength we needed to carry on.

In my hand was a letter addressed to Prime Minister John Major, outlining the reason for our hunger-strike, but, despite the cameras and reporters, he seemed reluctant to appear.

Recently, we had discovered that the fund set up to provide for our needs would soon be exhausted! Instead of lasting our lifetime, reports showed that money was drying up and the future looked bleak. The out of court settlement was supposed to see us through the rest of our lives, but then our life expectancy was unofficially estimated to be 18 and here we all were, in our mid-thirties showing every intention of living as long as anyone. We had to take our own futures in our hands and fight the only way we could for a fair settlement.

After statements to the press, we boarded the lift en route to Whitehall. As we shared the lift, Peter Robinson talked earnestly to me. He explained to me that we had achieved our goal by drawing all the national media to publicise our cause. It was time to call an end to the hunger strike he reasoned, but I wasn't so sure. Peter told me then, something I sensed he was reluctant to tell me. He was desperate to convince me to see sense. My mother had written to him earlier in the week, he wouldn't disclose the exact contents of the letter, but from what he did tell me it was suddenly clear to me exactly how worried and concerned my family were about the state of my health. His eyes seemed to plead with me to be reasonable. There was, he said no more to be gained by continuing to put our bodies through even one more day of starvation. One of the reporters outside Downing Street had shouted to me ...

"Kim! Are you prepared to die for your campaign?"

I had answered, "Yes I am!"

At the time I truly believed I would be prepared to die, but what would that do to my family?

As I began to realise the enormity of what I had taken on, a picture of my three children came into sharp focus. How could I even think of leaving them without a mother? How could I leave Eddie without a wife? He had given me his full support since the start of the campaign. Even though it was time-consuming and meant my usual family commitments had been neglected at times. Now here I was almost a stone lighter that I had been ten days earlier looking like I was about to fade away at any moment.

I decided right there and then that Peter had given me good advice and I would be a fool to put my children and Eddie through any more anxiety. I would fight on for the Thalidomide Action Group, but I needed to be strong and healthy with a clear head if I was to do any good!

We arrived a Whitehall where we had a meeting with Baronness Cumberledge. She listened to our requests and was sympathetic but unable to promise anything.

Peter took Heather, Freddie and myself and Eddie to the House of Commons restaurant to celebrate our success in bringing the campaign to the media's attention. Heather took a lot of convincing to agree to come off her hunger strike, she had been on hers for 14 days! Eventually she agreed with me, and Freddie reluctantly conceded as going it alone seemed futile. I ordered soup, scampi and chips with apple pie and custard for afters. I felt I could eat a horse, but I actually did little justice to my meal as my stomach had shrunk and wasn't ready for the onslaught!

As we said our goodbyes, Heather, Freddie and myself vowed to keep up the pressure on Guinness to listen to our requests and to look into the possibility of compensation for the victims of Thalidomide. It would be a long hard haul, Guinness was a huge company with all the resources at its beck and call. We were three disabled ordinary people living on very limited incomes, but our hearts were fiercely willing to fight for what we believed in.

When I arrived home, the relief was clearly visible on my three beautiful children's faces, as they talked and chatted to me about seeing me on television. The pride in their voices made my spirits soar. The will to go on grew stronger as I glowed in the warmth of my family circle.

I found it difficult to settle down to sleep that night, as my mind returned to the circumstances which had led to the events of the day in Downing Street.

In January 1994, I phoned Freddie Astbury in Liverpool to lend him my support as I had seen the news that day with a report about him and two others who were planning to take on the mighty Guinness company in search of compensation. (Guinness had bought over the DISTILLERS company, the original distributer of DISTAVAL). I had been upset about a recent documentary about Brazilian children who were being born with 'amphibian-like' limbs! This was how some papers had described the deformities caused by DISTAVAL over thirty years ago. I could hardly believe what I was hearing!

"O God, please don't let it happen all over again!" I cried out loud.

I held my head in my hands and wept, my heart was breaking. I sobbed until I became angry.

"I can't sit here and let this pass!" I decided.

The phone rang, it was my sister Beatrice. She was deeply upset at what she had just seen on television. She could barely talk, she was so emotional. That evening, I had several calls from my family and friends, all emotional, all devastated, all saying:

"How can this happen again?"

Thalidomide was supposed to have been banned after the devastation it had caused in the 60's. Over 4000 children had been born in Britain, but according to a professor, only one in ten of the babies with severe deformities had survived their first year of life. Indeed only 459 official thalidomide children are alive in Britain today.

Now I had witnessed a television documentary which had proof that thalidomide was being used in Brazil for various treatments including leprosy! There was a new generation of babies being born into the world with horrible deformities, I could scarcely allow myself to believe it!

I began to draw as much attention as possible to the plight of these unfortunate children. I contacted the local papers, I called the television news. For a while things were going well, but a visit to the Brazilian Embassy in London ended any hope I ever had of getting anyone to change the way Brazil policed their drug distribution. The Embassy denied anything was wrong with their country's policy on drugs. After frustrating debate and consultation with others, I realised I would be wasting my time pursuing my fight against Thalidomide in Brazil.

Meanwhile, more information was filtering through to me about the exact state of the 'Thalidomide Trust Fund'. Money was being depleted at an alarming rate, and as things were going, it appeared funds would be non-existent before most of us had reached our forties.

To understand how inadequate the 'settlement' was from the original distributors, DISTILLERS, the details need to be put into context.

In 1973, after years of wrangling and debate, the Thalidomide Trust was set up with an out of court settlement with total resources of £22 million. This figure was based on an unofficial assumption that most of us would probably never marry as our life expectancy was unlikely to average 18 years. In actual fact, most of us had married and had children. Lately evidence was coming to show that a second generation of similar deformities was affecting the children of the original thalidomide victims!

Although we each receive an annual income from the Trust, it is not ready cash as many people assume. To receive money from the Trust, we have to make a request for a specific amount for a specific item. If the board of Trustees agree it is absolutely necessary, the cheque is sent off for the amount complete with 35% tax deducted. No provision is made for any dependants which in the case of many male victims meant they were unable to provide for their family. They were surviving on state benefits. Coupled with the fact that the trust fund was due to run dry very soon, I felt something had to be done.

Within the space of a week, I was deputy chairperson of the 'Thalidomide Action Group'. I determined myself that I would not rest until full provision was made for all victims. Through no fault of our own, we had been put in a position where we needed extraordinary help just to lead a normal life. DISTILLERS had been bought over by Guinness, and Thalidomide was being distributed in third world countries, albeit branded as another name. The risk was still there, and huge profits were being made. Something was very wrong, and I could not help myself as the urge to campaign for a realistic compensation payment drove me to the steps of 10 Downing Street, and almost to my death. Where was I going to get the strength from for the long battle I knew lay before me?

Chapter Two

How will we afford seven pairs of shoes?

Mum had just bought me a new pair of shoes. I was ready to begin nursery school and I was really excited. I was a big girl now!

My eldest brother Alex was in P4, he was eight. Frances my elder sister was in P3, she was seven, Trevor next to me in age, was in P2. It would soon by my 3rd Birthday. We Rodgers all went to nursery school at three years old, it was fast becoming a tradition! Sitting beside me on the cover of the pram, was my younger sister Elizabeth, she was only 19th months old. Under the covers of the pram lay Joan the latest arrival, at only 7 months old - she had no interest in nursery just yet but it was the only thing I could think of! Hallowe'en coming, and as soon as school opened for new term I could start nursery!

A few days later Mum was busy with the usual morning rush trying to get six children organised for the day, when she felt ill. The doctor sent her into hospital for tests and a neighbour minded us all for a while, until Daddy was able to get home from the Shipyard where he worked. Daddy looked after us while Mum had to stay in hospital for a day or two.

"When is Mummy coming back home?" I asked.

"Your Mummy will be home soon Beatrice, don't worry, you be a good girl and help your brothers and sisters and the doctors will send Mummy home as good as new," Dad soothed.

In hospital, the doctors had diagnosed an infection in her urinary tract. Mum was sleeping throughout the day, she was so tired. Maybe she was making the most of the peace and quiet before she had to return to Fort Apache! In the late evening, a young nurse asked Mum why she wasn't sleeping.

"You'll get me into trouble with the sister, everyone on the ward has to be asleep," she chastened.

"Would you like me to give you something to help you sleep?" she asked.

Mum replied no, she had slept all day and was hoping to go home the next day and didn't want to feel dozy. Later the nurse came back, and on seeing Mum still awake, repeated her earlier warning. Mum relented to keep the young nurse happy, and was administered two Distaval to help her sleep.

Weeks later, there was a buzz in our house. We were going to have a new baby brother or sister in the Summer! We joked about the fact that there was no room left in our house for another baby. Alex and Trevor started to chant.

"We want a boy! We want a boy!"

We girls sang out,

"We want a girl! We want a girl!"

Mum and Dad quietened everyone down. The thunderous din was heard every night in our house. Six children all under eight years old could put your head in a spin. Now here we were getting ready for another one!

The day arrived, Mum had had a good pregnancy. Just as well, as she coped with six boisterous children. Dad was with Mum in the maternity ward but the nurse, knowing Dad had all of us to look after, sent him home telling him nothing world be happening for quite a while.

Dad left and rode home on his motorbike to look after us. He had just arrived home when the door knocked ... it was the Police.

Mad rush and panic, no one was available to look after us. Alex, being the oldest was told by Dad that he was in charge of the 'wee ones'. Daddy disappeared. We all behaved ourselves that night. There was no boisterous din in our house that night. Something was wrong with our Mummy. Even Elizabeth and baby Joan were quiet, except for the on-going questions:

"Where's my Mummy? Where's our new baby?"

At the hospital, no one mentioned to Mum that there was anything to worry about. She was hurriedly moved into a ward where a nurse broke a capsule in half and gave it to Mum to 'help her sleep'/

As Mum woke in a daze the doctor was standing at her bedside.

"Is my baby okay?" Mum asked.

"You have a little girl," replied the doctor.

"I'm afraid there is a problem with your baby Mrs. Rodgers (Mum was drifting in and out of consciousness) ... she has no thumb."

"How would she be able to hold a pencil or a spoon to feed herself?" Mum mumbled before she drifted off into a drug-induced sleep.

As Dad arrived at the hospital, the doctor spoke to him and explained that his baby daughter had deformities which would make walking impossible. She also had no thumb. Dad was devastated, bewildered, he wanted to know what had gone wrong? The pregnancy had been normal, the birth was perfectly normal too. The doctor explained that the baby Rodgers heart and all internal organs were in perfect condition. In the air hung an unspoken question, although the innuendo was almost palatable. Did they want this child home with them?

"She's our daughter, she's coming home with us!" my Dad insisted.

Dad rode home in a daze. He had a motor bike at that time, to save on bus fares to and from work at the Shipyard where he worked shifts. His mind was in turmoil. In his distressed state, he put a lit cigarette into his coat pocket. The cigarette burned a hole right though into his skin. He didn't even notice, he had another pain deep down inside him much stronger than physical pain. Tears streamed down his cheeks as realisation hit him. His daughter was seriously disabled, there was not a thing in the world he could do about it, life would never be the same again.

Mum left hospital the next day. New mothers usually had a week long stay in maternity wards, but our baby sister was 'having tests' so it was best for everyone if Mum went home and "the baby would follow later when they had completed their examinations," the doctor said. A nurse showed our baby sister to Mum wrapped up in a little planet through a glass partition, before she left for home. Mum still in a little disorientated from the previous day, looked at her baby and wept. She looked just like all her other children, even if she had no thumb, she'd manage! Mum determined.

Mum and Dad visited the hospital just once before our baby sister came home. Again she was wrapped in a blanket, while a nurse hovered in the background. Dad had spoken to Mum only briefly about the problem and in his effort not to hurt Mum had only skimmed over the mention of 'walking difficulties'. Perhaps he knew if he said it out loud, it would become too real to cope with.

On the day Mum arrived home from hospital, we were so pleased to see her, we all wanted to sit on her knee at once! Dad explained that our new baby sister couldn't come home yet. For a while we teased the boys because 'there were going to be five girls against two boys' but the joking stopped as Dad gathered us all around him. As we kneeled on the floor, we were transfixed on Dad's every word. Mum was sitting behind us, and couldn't see our faces as we heard that our baby sister had something wrong with her and couldn't walk. Silence, a rare commodity in our house, hung in the air. Tears filled our eyes as the reality hit us. Only Alex, the oldest, really understood. In an instant he swivelled his head around to look at Mum. Mum says she will never forget the look on his face, a mixture of pain, concern, and total disbelief, and something else she couldn't explain. From that day Alex spoke with a very profound stammer.

Being the chatterbox and very inquisitive, I said, "Daddy she will be able to walk a little tiny bit won't she, and maybe when she's a big girl like me she will learn to walk."

"I don't know Beatrice, let's hope so" Dad said trying to keep his emotions in check.

Mum was quizzed by Social Services. They asked all sorts of questions. "Do you drink whiskey? Can you think of any reason why your baby should be born like this?"

They asked so many questions, it was obvious they were trying to find someone to blame for the way our sister had been born. Meanwhile, local shop keepers and leading residents in our family were being asked what kind of family we were, and what kind of parents Mum and Dad were! The consultant in charge of the Maternity ward had decided to find out if Mum and Dad were capable of looking after 'a special child'. Such a baby could not be allowed home to an irresponsible family!

Mum and Dad must have passed "the test", as our baby sister arrived home six days later. By that time, the neighbours had heard that she was different, but I don't think anyone was quite prepared for what they saw when she arrived.

We were being looked after by a neighbour when they arrived home. Up until then the nurses had done everything for our baby, now it was up to Mum to take care of her. Mum started to change her nappy. As Mum pulled back the blanket, she saw for the first time the full horror of her baby daughter's condition. She reeled in shock, why hadn't anyone told her? She looked at Dad with disbelief and helplessness. Dad couldn't believe his own eyes, nothing could have prepared them for this! He ran into the bedroom where he cried until he could cry no more.

We arrived home full of excitement. We wanted to see our sister! Mum told us she was calling her KIM and somehow it sounded just perfect for such a cutie! Kim was wrapped in blankets, as all babies are when they come out of hospital for the first time. As Mum pulled the covers back, we saw Kim for the first time.

Her tiny arms were shortened by what looked like an elbow where her wrist should have been. Her legs were curled up into perfect little pink feet, where her knees should have been. There was no thumb on one hand, and two of her fingers were stuck together. She had the brightest smile any of us had ever seen, and we soon forgot about her different arms and legs as we gazed with delight at her beautiful little pink face! Here she was, home at last, where she belonged!

CHAPTER THREE

Kim's 'first steps'

Some neighbours called to see Kim. I remember feeling angry because they were making 'awkward' remarks, couldn't they see that my sister was shining with life and beauty?

From the day Kim was born, she was a fighter. What she lacked in physical perfection, she more than made up for in sheer determination!

At six months old, the hospital made what we called 'the flower pot'. It was actually a plaster of paris from Kim's waist to her ankles, and she rolled about the floor like any other baby of her age. At nine months old, the 'rocker board' was made and Kim was strapped into it. It consisted of a square board with two leather straps and a stabiliser rod to hold Kim upright. One waist-belt was secured and two footstraps held her feet down toward the board. Again, she twisted and wriggled trying to get on the move. The natural instinct to walk was as strong as with any child. There was no doubt about it our little sister was going to walk!

As Kim became older, the artificial limbs became more and more complex. There were endless visits to the Musgrave Park Hospital, where they had specialist knowledge in the making of artificial limbs for patients who had undergone amputation.

The technicians were fascinated by the strong will and spirit of Kim. They went to great lengths to please her, and she knew exactly what she wanted, and what she didn't want! She soon let them know when anything caused her discomfort! There were numerous visits and adjustments before a completed pair of limbs were ready. Some of the work was painstaking for everyone concerned, after all, the technicians had never made limbs for children so small, with such unusual disabilities.

Outside, in the big, bad world, the papers were beginning to print headlines about the recent spate of babies born with unusual deformities.

'DRUG BABIES'! screamed one paper. Few facts were known at this stage, and many cruel stories were written. Many people in their ignorance assumed that the babies written about were being born to mothers who were drug addicts! This only added to the burden for most parents as they tried to cope with their children, day to day.

Our local paper carried a heartbreaking letter from one woman, who was struggling with a daughter with almost identical disabilities to Kim's.

"If there are any other mothers out there with a child like mine, please contact me!" she pleaded.

The realisation that our family wasn't going through the nightmare of not knowing what had happened to cause Kim's condition somehow gave us hope, although we began to sense something more sinister to come.

At home, life was going on as usual. Mum and Dad had started doing exercises with Kim every day. Their aim was to lengthen out Kim's arms and legs, so hopefully fewer operations would be necessary in the future. It was Dad's own idea, and he was relentless as he encouraged Kim to keep going. It was for her own good he insisted.

Every night before bed, Dad would hold Kim up in his arms and make Kim pull herself up with the strength of her own arms. It was hard work, but the determination showed in her face as she repeated them over and over again. Soon her arms reappeared less twisted, the exercises were working.

Once, my Grandfather came to visit. Kim was in the middle of her usual exercise routine. Grandad gave my Dad a real telling off, he said it was cruel to put Kim through such an ordeal.

"Don't do that to the poor wee crater, leave her alone!" he shouted.

As Dad tried to explain what he was trying to do, Grandad showed his utter disgust by storming off. It broke Dad's heart to put Kim through her paces every night, especially when she was tired, but their perseverance paid off!

To all of us at home, Kim was perfectly normal except she had to wear 'walkies' as we affectionately called her artificial limbs. Hardly a day went by when she wouldn't have her limbs on. She had to get used to wearing them. Elizabeth, Joan and I played with Kim and watched over her carefully. We had to, she was a real daredevil! Mum always told us not to treat Kim differently, she was allowed to join in with everything we played. Kim certainly knew what she wanted to do. What a strong character she was! She ruled us all and had us wrapped around her little finger. When we played 'house', Kim insisted on being 'Mummy'. She wore Mum's shoes on her hands instead of her feet, she looked so comical! As she crawled about playing with her sisters and brothers, Kim was at her happiest. With us, she was just another kid charging about full of energy. There was nothing she couldn't do once she put her mind to it. Without her artificial legs, she could be herself, she ran about as fast as any of us.

"Race you!" she would shout.

Whenever she felt she was losing the race, she would hook her arm around your ankle, down you went! She was a real scamp! but we laughed at her antics. Without her limbs Kim could be free. It's hard to imagine wheat it must be like to have your legs and feet encased in leather and metal, with your waist strapped to a metal rod. Kim wore her limbs every day and she was a master at walking, she had it down to a fine art.

Outside the cosy comfort of home, parents were meeting at an afternoon 'playgroup' set up by the local hospital for children with deformities like Kim's. While some children rolled about the floor, others zoomed about on their limbs, to the amazement of various experts, watching the children's every move. They scribbled notes fervently and marvelled at just how adept the children were at getting about.

Some children had no legs, others had hands growing straight out of their shoulders, but had normal legs. Some hand neither arms nor legs, just tiny feet and one or two fingers jutting out from their shoulders, while their feet appeared to come out of their abdomen. These children didn't have 'normal' deformities, they all had obvious similarities. While doctors watched fascinated by the skills and ingenuity of their children, the parents were having discussions of their own. They had formed the basis of a committee, they needed to find answers as to why they were all here with children who appeared to have been born in very similar circumstances. They vowed to stand together until the truth was discovered. Already they had started to put some evidence together.

One mother had been given two DISTAVAL to sedate her after she had arrived at her father's home to find him lying dead. Her mother, sister and herself were each given the tablets as a sedative. A couple of weeks later she found out she was pregnant. Her son was born with only fingers were his shoulders were. Mum had been given two DISTAVAL during her short stay in hospital, 'to help her sleep'. A couple of weeks later she discovered she was expecting Kim. The stories were all similar, someone somewhere would have answers to their questions.

This was an unknown phenomenon, doctors were fumbling in the dark for answers and solutions. The limb-fitting centre was having trouble fitting some of the children. They were used to dealing with amputee 'stumps'. In the early days deformed arms or legs had been amputated! Some parents after agonising agreed and the operations were performed. Mum and Dad would not agree. When Kim was old enough she could make up her own mind. Dad said to the doctors.

"You make the artificial limbs fit Kim, you're not going to make my daughter fit your artificial limbs!"

The doctor's couldn't have possibly known how ingenious the children would be at adapting their deformed limbs to everyday tasks. It was a wonder to watch how some of the children played ordinary games with extraordinary skills. Those without hands or arms did amazing contortionist movements with their legs and mouths. Those without legs made up for the deficiency with feats of strength using their arms!

There was no holding back nature. These children had never known what it was like to have normal arms or legs, so they used what they had to perform every day tasks.

When Christian Barnard succeeded with his first heart transplant, I remember asking Kim;

"What would you do if Christian Barnard could make you a pair of real legs?"

"I wouldn't know what to do with them, I'd feel weird" Kim answered logically.

Another weekly event brought all the children together. A local businessman heard about Kim from a neighbour who worked for him as a housekeeper. He lived in a large house on the prosperous Malone Road. He offered to let the children and their families have use of his private swimming pool on Saturday mornings.

To help Kim stay afloat, a costume was made with pockets sewn in to insert eight polystyrene floats. We all looked forward to going to the big house on Saturdays. The other children fascinated us. We were used to Kim, but here were more children the same, but not the same. The range of disabilities was unbelievable. They were all game for anything and we had a lot of fun.

As Kim progressed there were a few frights for us, she was always kidding around and dropping into the water like a stone. Eventually the floats were removed one by one until the costume had all the pockets empty. Now Kim wanted a REAL swimming costume, but not like one any of us had, O No ... Kim wanted a bikini! We collapsed into giggles as she shook her little hips and sang,

"Anything you can do, I can do better, I can do anything better than you!"

Once again, Kim made 'wee buns' out of something we had never dared hope she could accomplish.

CHAPTER FOUR

The climbing frame

The time was fast approaching, when Kim would be old enough to begin nursery school. Mum was anxious about Kim asking questions as to why she wasn't going. After all, Elizabeth and Joan went every day and Kim went with Mum to pick them up in the afternoons. She was eagerly looking forward to starting just as I had done three years previously. One afternoon while Mum was waiting outside the nursery doors with all the other Mums, the school principal came by.

"And when will this little Miss Rodgers be joining our nursery?" Mr Campbell asked with a friendly smile.

Mum looked embarrassed as she replied

"O Kim can't go to nursery"

"And why not? he asked.

"Kim's disabled and can't go to a normal school" Mum said getting embarrassed as the other mothers looked on in amusement.

"Kim can walk, can't she?"

"Yes, she can indeed!" Mum said proudly.

"Well then! we'll expect to see Kim bright and early at the start of next term!" he insisted.

Off he went leaving Mum with a broad smile on her face.

Summer holidays came and went, and Mum was busy getting all the uniforms organised. Joan was starting her second year at nursery, so Kim would have someone looking out for her.

On the first day Kim was made welcome. Mum told the teacher she wanted Kim to be treated just the same as the others. One teacher who taught at the other section objected to Kim being placed. She tried to advise the other teachers not to take on the responsibility of looking after Kim. Fortunately they were quite happy to have Kim in their class. Mum was deeply upset when she heard about the incident, and had shed tears as any Mum does when their youngest starts school. The incident stabbed at her heart, was this the start of taunts and cruel remarks for her daughter? What way would the other children treat her if one teacher had such an attitude?

When the time came to collect Kim and Joan, Mum was anxious. The teacher called Mum to one side.

"Kim is one special wee girl, the others love her, she's so full of beans, she wants to take part in everything! She's going to get along just fine" she said.

In the playground at our nursery school stood a metal climbing frame. Every child who ever attended Taughmonagh Nursery climbed that frame dozens of time during their stay. It was tradition. Every day at playtime, Kim would try to climb the frame. Her limbs were awkward and stiff. She had to pull herself up with the strength in her arms. She failed day after day. Every day she had another go, others were climbing to the top and singing

"I'm the king of the castle, get down! you dirty rascal!"

Joan offered to push Kim up to the first bar, the first bar was where you could swing head over feet and flip over your own head, it was great fun. Kim fumed;

"Leave me alone, I can do it all by myself!"

"I'll only lift you up to the first bar" Joan reasoned.

"I don't want you to help me!" Kim bellowed.

Kim grabbed her right limb and pulled at it with all her might to haul it up on to the first bar. Then she pulled herself up over the bar with her belly. With the strength in her little short arms she pulled high enough to swing the other heavy limb up, so her foot was on the bar. Using both arms to straighten herself, she held her balance and yelled for everyone to hear;

"I'm the king of the ca-astle, now get DOWN you dirty ra-ascal!!"

When we heard what she had done, we were so delighted we ran about the house that night like a tribe of wild indians! Our baby sister had climbed the 'frame'. It was like an initiation ceremony, and she had passed with flying colours! Seven Rodgers' had attended and succeeded in conquering that frame, Kim was no different! The next day Kim did 'the flip'. The teacher nearly done a flip when she saw her!

For two years, Kim sailed through nursery school. The nursery section was separate form the rest of the main school building. The young three and four year-olds had been curious at first but came to accept Kim as their equal. Now she had to make the transition to Primary level where the five to eleven year-olds roamed the corridors making fun of anyone who wore spectacles or had sticking out ears. In fact, anything considered out of the 'norm' was ridiculed and poked fun at. Kim was going into a big pond with big fish, and some of them were predators!

Kim's first day at Taughmonagh school was a special day in all our lives. There had already been 6 Rodgers' through the gates. Alex had just left to attend Secondary school. Frances was in P7, Trevor in P6, I was in P4, Elizabeth P3, Joan P2 and Kim was right behind her starting P1. Her teacher was Mrs Bronte, a jolly friendly woman who seemed genuinely pleased to have Kim in her class. She often talked to Mum about Kim's progress and took Kim to after school activities. Mrs Bronte held Scripture Union classes at lunch-time and Kim attended. She loved her first teacher.

Mum had started a job in the school kitchen as a dinner lady, so all in all things were sailing along nicely.

In the playground, the girls played german-skips. Lots of elastic bands were knotted together to form a full circle. Two girls stood end to end with the elastic around their ankles holding it taut. The aim of the game was to jump over the line and lift the line to form a cross. Then you had to jump out of the way of the band before it caught your feet. As usual, Kim had to join in. She was happily skipping away (on all fours, Elizabeth, Kim's personal slave and keeper of the Royal limbs had removed them at her Majesty's request.)

Our school principal walked by and paused to watch Kim. She was oblivious to him as she jumped and swung to shout "YO!" in triumph. When she realised he was watching her she put her hand up to her mouth and said

"Oops!"

Kim knew she was supposed to keep her limbs on all day in school. (Mum and Dad's rule, not the schools') Mr Campbell stood towering over her 6'4" tall and smiled as he waved his finger to show mock disapproval. His eyes shone with pride and admiration. He had a lot to be proud of. Hadn't he insisted my sister join his school? Now here she was having a great time mixing with all the other children happy as a sandboy!

~ •~

Printed below, is a letter which appeared in Where magazine in September, 1966. The letter, written by my mother is about Kim, to keep her privacy, Mum called her 'Jane'.

We reprint below a letter sent to WHERE by the mother of a thalidomide child. She makes a simple point: that all kinds of handicapped children should not be classed together as needing special education. She offers the experience of her legless daughter Jane, who has made a courageous and encouraging start at a normal school.

I am writing in the hope that hearing about my little girl's progress at nursery school will broaden the outlook for the education authorities in England. Unfortunately no other child like Jane has benefited here in Northern Ireland. My little girl is what is officially known as a Thalidomide child. She has to wear artificial legs and has severely deformed arms and hands. But I'm happy to add, her hands are no handicap to her. Two fingers on one hand (right) and four on the other one are as useful to her as a complete pair of hands is to you and me.

When so much publicity was given to these children, we the parents, were invited to inspect the 'special' school for handicapped children. During our visit to the school, we were told that the school was meant for 25 children. At the time it had 74 children from 7-17 years old. We were also informed that there was a long waiting list for a place. My husband and I agreed there and then that if it was possible, we would go all out for a normal school placing for Jane, rather than deprive a more unfortunate child of a place in the specially equipped school.

The first step

We have seven children, and the first six went to nursery school. My husband and I are of the opinion that this is a very necessary part of a child's education. We are naturally anxious that our children should get as good an education as our Government can offer. One day, when I was leaving my second youngest daughter in nursery school, the headmaster approached me and asked if I was going to allow Jane to attend when she became three years old. I was very surprised to put it mildly, for we had worried about the problem since Jane was born.

I could not possibly write down all that happened since that day, but when the time came, against all advice and warnings given by both medical and education officials, the headmaster and teacher welcomed our child to the nursery. She fitted in right away and after the teacher and other children got over the stage of treating Jane like a china doll everything went along fine. After only a few weeks the teacher reported, that really, she had less trouble with Jane than some of the other children.

All the problems we were looking for sorted themselves out, and far from upsetting the other 24 children, Jane's presence seemed to bring out the best in them. Some mothers who were asked to watch for a change in their child's attitude reported a change for the better. None of the children worried about Jane or pitied her.

After eight weeks her walking appliance had to be changed. It was a big change which the specialist said should not have come for at least another year, but Jane was ready for it. Unfortunately as a result, Jane lost confidence in her teacher's ability to take her to the toilet. Twice she soiled her pants. The young teacher (this was her first teaching job) was the type of person who couldn't cope with this situation so she asked for help. The only help offered was the order to take Jane from nursery school and send her to a school specially started for Thalidomide children.

As I am just a layman on any important subject it is quite possible that I was wrong, but it is my opinion that it is unfair to try to educate armless children with legless ones. It just wouldn't be fair to expect a little boy with no arms to compete with a girl like Jane. I know all the children personally who would be at the school, so I know the problems there are. We objected very strongly to this solution to the problem, for we knew that Jane was of 'clean habits' from an early age so it was just a matter of the teacher regaining the child's confidence.

Left where she was happy

The officer of health was approached on our behalf and agreed to visit the nursery when Jane was present. He was delighted with her progress and said that an individual child could not be assessed and put into schools A, B or C without someone first meeting the child. The result was, Jane was left where she was happy, and within a few days of her starting back to routine she asked her teacher to take her to the toilet. (I should have mentioned that taking the child to the toilet was the only special attention that was needed of the teacher and she had agreed to do this.)

Because of well-meaning friends advising her not to take on such a responsibility in her first probation year, the teacher had expected and was prepared for a really difficult job. Now, after seven months, she can still hardly believe how well everything has worked out. She realised all eyes were on her, waiting for the first sign of failure, so naturally it was a few weeks before she could relax and treat Jane for what she is - a normal intelligent child who unfortunately has to walk on artificial legs.

Helping other children

I only wish that more headmasters and teachers would make an effort to help the children who are not so severely handicapped instead of classing them all the same. Two little boys I know have hands the same as Jane, but are quite normal in every way - as yet there are no signs of them being educated at ordinary primary schools. If only someone else could see Jane at school and offer to take some other child into their care.

I hope I haven't given the impression that there were no problems at all, but if a young teacher can overcome these, surely more experienced teachers can try? A new climbing frame was installed in the nursery last week, and to everyone's amazement Jane climbed to the top. The frame is about four feet high so this is quite an achievement. It has given us hope that she will be able to manage five steps up to each classroom when she goes to primary school!

CHAPTER FIVE

Sunday best

The Thalidomide Committee members were busy with meetings. More parents had joined, some were still reluctant. Some parents still had not recovered from the shock of having their son or daughter born disabled. They wanted to be left alone, they had enough problems without trying to do battle with a huge company, it was a waste of time they said.

All the while, expenses were mounting. With such special needs, many parents were finding the going tough. Kim was getting through 2-3 dresses a week! Mum was having to patch the knees of her dresses, as crawling about soon wore them into holes. Luckily, she had four older sisters to pass on hand-me-downs, but even at that the supply was fast running out. Mum started sewing. She would make 5 dresses at a time. While we were asleep in bed, Mum was running the sewing machine, if she wasn't making a new dress, she was patching one for Kim.

Our new dresses were always kept for 'Sunday Best'. On Sunday mornings Mum and Dad liked to have a lie in. Well that was the theory, but they rarely got the chance, as our house was like a mad house every Sunday morning. We girls all slept together in a big cast iron bed. Frances and myself at the top end of the bed, while Elizabeth, Joan and Kim slept at the bottom end. There were legs everywhere! (well almost).

Every Sunday morning, Alex and Trevor would come into our room and challenge us to a pillow fight. We took it in turns to be 'swiper'. One of us would jump up and down on top of the bed while another would try to swipe at your ankles, and bring you down with a crescending thud on the mattress. We had the best fun. Alex, being the oldest, was the best at getting you 'out'. We each had a go, and Kim was no exception. The only problem was, once Kim was 'in' we couldn't get her 'out'.

She jumped all over the bed on all fours, so it was impossible to swipe at her ankles. We protested loudly of course, then Kim would stand and heave herself up and down by lifting her shoulders.

"Look, I can't jump like this" she would say with a pathetic look on her face. (Pasted on for special effect.)

'O alright!' we'd sing out in unison.

Kim went back on all fours, and straight into another giggling session.

The only way to get her 'out' was to try to catch her on the turn with one almighty swipe by swinging at her rear-end, so she flipped over and on to her back. Alex would grasp the pillow with both hands and shake all the feathers down to one end. Brandishing the pillow like a swashbuckler, he would shout;

"She's going down! She's history!"

All seven of us giggled until we almost cried as Kim and Alex went into battle. Kim scuttled all over the bed ducking and diving to avoid the mighty pillow. Alex's face was a picture of determination as he swiped at Kim. Of course, when Kim was finally put 'out' she protested loudly that Alex hadn't gone for her ankles. Mum and Dad would call out at regular intervals for us to be quiet and get back into bed. But they knew we were having a whale of a time and rarely ever actually came near us to spoil our fun. Mind you, if Kim was put 'out' too soon for her liking, she sometimes took 'the hump' and scuttled off into Mum and Dad's room to spoil their fun!

After breakfast, we all had a bath and dressed in our Sunday best clothes for Sunday school. Earlier that week, Mum had bought Kim a new furry hood with pom-poms and a matching muffler, it was so cute on her. It was especially for Kim to start Sunday school. She tried it on for us all to see, she was really looking forward to joining the rest of us now she was old enough. However, she wasn't able to go that morning, as Mum had bumped into our minister a few days earlier.

While at the post office, Mum saw our minister,

"Kim is really looking forward to starting Sunday school" Mum told him.

"I'm sorry Mrs Rodgers, there's no room in our classes for Kim." he replied.

"What do you mean, no room? All of my children were christened in your church, and they all attend Sunday school in your church." Mum said, preparing herself for a big disappointment.

"We simply do not have the facilities for a child like Kim," he said.

"I see what you mean Reverend, don't worry, Kim won't be attending your church I know exactly what you are trying to say, I've heard it all before. Didn't Jesus once say 'suffer little children'" Mum replied, feeling more anger than she could handle. The minister mumbled something about Mum taking things the wrong way, but Mum hurried off, the tears stinging her eyes. How would she tell Kim she couldn't go with the rest of us come Sunday morning?

Another minister, however, was more than happy for Kim to attend his church. So Kim, Joan and Elizabeth all went to the big white church on the local green every Sunday. Alex, Frances, Trevor and I still attended our own church as we were in the middle of confirmation studies. Eventually, we all left, as it never felt the same. Somehow the message of the church didn't ring true to us any more, not in that particular church anyway.

Kim joined the brownies and any other activity she could get into. The church on the green had all sorts of fun days organised and Kim was involved in the lot!

It wasn't long before our faith was restored though. One day our door knocked. I opened the door to find the tallest man I'd ever seen.

"Is your mother in dear child?" he asked in a soft tone.

As I stood and stared at this tall man smiling with the twinkliest eyes, he said

"And what is your name little lady?"

"Beatrice" I answered still captured by his smile.

"What a beautiful name" he exclaimed. "Is your mother home?"

He reached out his huge hand and shook my hand. I drew myself away reluctantly, I was fascinated by the presence and charm of this huge man. I went to call Mum. We all followed Mum out to the door and gathered around her skirt trying to get a good view of this stranger at our door. Mum invited the friendly 'giant' into our home. He sat down on the sofa, it dwarfed beneath him.

He introduced himself as Reverend Harvey from McCracken Memorial Church on the Malone Road. (A very prosperous and up-market part of town.) He said he liked to call from time to time on all the families in our area to play street games with the children. Would Mum mind if he called occasionally to take us out? He marvelled at the sight of us all gathered around Mum and made it his business to speak to everyone of us individually. He was genuinely interested in all of us and said we were

"A marvellous little family" he enthused.

Through all our childhood, the memories he gave to all of us were simply some of the best a child could have!

At Christmas, he would take us all out to tea and scones (when I say all I mean practically the whole street) not just the Rodgers clan! Every family in our area knew Reverend Harvey, he was a legend in his own lifetime. When he arrived, all the children would gather around his car, he would fit as many children as possible into his car, and off we would go on a mystery tour always fun, always safe. He took us to the local old peoples' home, which was situated in one of the most beautiful rose garden parks in the country. There we would sing Christmas carols to the delight of the residents. Kim sang like a bird, and never failed to draw attention. One elderly resident was moved to tears as Kim sang one verse solo of 'O little town of Bethlehem'. We felt like film-stars when we left the residents glowing with all the joys of Christmas. Good old Reverend Harvey, he seemed to have such a caring way of making everyone feel wonderful in any situation!

In summer, every day was viewed with anticipation. Would Reverend Harvey come around? When he arrived to cheers from the children, he would play a game where he threw a brand new tennis ball in the air. Whoever caught the ball could keep it. Everyone wanted to catch that ball. When it was won, we weren't disappointed for long, there was a large bag of them! Reverend Harvey said the people in the local sports shop gave him a special discount because he bought so many of them. When he ran out of balls, he would borrow a ball back, and keep throwing it and giving sixpence to the one who caught it. Everyone's a winner with Rev. Harvey!

There were trips to Downpatrick with a running commentary about local history. We hung on his every word. The "Giant's Ring" was an ancient monument he took us to on several occasions. We had picnics, and ran all the way around the hedges bordering the monument. There were other trips, too numerous to mention, and throughout all of them Rev. Harvey would compliment each and everyone of us regularly. He encouraged us to learn and enjoy our youth. He was the nicest person we had ever met, a true man of God.

He had a big influence in our lives, especially Kim's, she adored him. He treated her the same way he treated everyone ... as if she was the most special person in all the world.

CHAPTER SIX

Putting the boot in!

Wherever Kim went, she was fiercely independent. At school, everyone was used to her, especially anyone who had offered to help on a
previous occasion. Even if she had fallen over she would refuse help.
Sometimes she would smile and politely refuse and say thank you,
other times she would not be so polite! Then she would proceed to
haul herself up with whatever was available to her. One day, Kim fell
badly, and the metal rod of the right side limb skewered deeply into
her right thigh, leaving a gaping hole. Mum rushed out horrified at
the blood gushing, but Kim sat and laughed much to the bewilder-
ment of all of us. Later we remembered watching a film called 'Reach
for the sky' starring Kenneth More. It was the life story of Douglas
Bader, a world war 2 pilot who had lost his legs and had artificial
limbs. He insisted on flying and was captured and sent to Colditz.
The Germans took his limbs away because he tried to escape so many
times! In the film, he laughed every time he fell. Dad had made a

point of bringing Kim in especially to watch the film. She was quieter than we have ever seen her, and was fascinated by the story. From then on, Kim laughed whenever she fell, and would never cry.

On one occasion Kim, aged five, fell over in the street. When she fell, she landed like a plank of wood due to the limbs, which meant she was usually hurt either physically or emotionally, especially if someone had seen her go down in such an ungainly fashion. A young man of about seventeen rushed over to help lift Kim up.

"Are you hurt love? Let me help you" he said.

"Take off!" Kim bellowed in frustration, "I can do it all by myself, leave me alone!"

The young man looked hurt and embarrassed, but watched (from afar) as Kim took a considerable time to haul herself up using the kerbside and a wooden fence for support. As he walked off, his smile showed admiration for the fiesty little girl, he wouldn't forget that 'little madam' in a hurry.

When Kim was eight, we moved house. The house was in an estate not far from the centre of Belfast, and though it was only 3 miles from our previous home, in those days it seemed like a hundred miles away. The new house had stairs, and we were all delighted to be living in a 'real' house. The stairs were a source of fun for us as our previous home had been a bungalow. Kim was delighted in bumping downstairs on her rear-end! It was a tribute to Kim that Mum and Dad didn't consider the stairs to be a problem for her.

Frances, our oldest sister once held a birthday party. I was allowed to stay downstairs as unpaid slave as I was old enough to serve food. Elizabeth, Joan and Kim were sent upstairs 'out of the way'. Just as the party was getting going, a courting couple made the unfortunate decision to sit on the stairs and have a necking session. The 'three wee ones' as they were affectionately known in the family, had been watching from the landing most of the evening. They hatched a fiendish plot with the use of Frances's own hand made creation. She had knitted herself a very long scarf like the one worn by 'Dr Who', a cult television character at the time. Elizabeth had tied a heavy army-style boot to the end. Joan and Elizabeth then held Kim over the stair-rail by the waist while Kim swung the boot like a pendulum at the unsuspecting couple! When Frances heard the fuss, she gave them a telling off only an older sister can give in a humiliated rage. The next day she laughed at the thought of it.

During this time, Kim received a splint which was designed to straighten her right arm. She had it strapped to her from the wrist to above the elbow, and was meant to wear it overnight. She hated that splint! Over a period of time, Joan became expert at removing the splint as soon as Kim, Elizabeth and she had gone to bed, and she awakened early every morning to replace it so Mum and Dad would not suspect anything. Meanwhile, Joan and Elizabeth gently pulled at Kim's arms to 'stretch' them so it would appear the splint was working! I caught then at it one evening as I passed the bedroom. The three of them were giggling and curiosity got the better of me. I walked in to find Elizabeth holding Kim while Joan pulled Kim by the wrist with great determination! No one ever told Mum about the splint, and the doctors seemed happy enough, so maybe it worked!

Around the same time, Kim was given a new wheelchair. When I saw it I hated it! It was navy blue with large cushions and small wheels, a typical type of chair at the time.

'I'm not pushing our Kim in that! people will think she's handicapped!" I wailed.

"No way! I'm not taking our Kim out in that!" Elizabeth echoed.

The reason for our childish outburst was simple. In our eyes Kim was perfectly normal. Pushing her around in a chair we had only ever seen 'spastic' or 'mentally retarded' adults sitting in, somehow made us feel angry, not for ourselves, but for Kim. Eventually, we had to give in, as Kim was too big for a pushchair and had to get to school and other longer journeys somehow.

We also had been on the receiving end of cruel remarks already, and young as we were, it hurt us to hear some of the things people would say.

"O what a lovely wee face, such a shame" was a common remark.

"Why doesn't your Mummy cover those legs with trousers?" was another.

When I heard that, I was angry. What did they mean? Did they think my sister should be grotesquely ugly as well as disabled? Did they mean her pretty face was wasted on her? Often I went home frustrated with anger, as we were brought up to respect our elders and not to answer back. I never spoke my mind, just smiled and walked off bumping the wheelchair up and down kerbs in frustration, Kim would laugh knowing I was annoyed and tell me off when I bumped one kerb too many!

Saturdays were busy for all of us. After breakfast, we were off to the cinema for the 'minors' matinee. We boarded a bus for the Lisburn Road where the 'Majestic' picture house was situated. Films like 'Old Mother Riley', 'Tarzan' and the obligatory 'childrens film' made especially for the matinees were shown. Mum gave us seven shillings, a shilling each to spend. Straight after the show, we walked up to the local park and swung around the maypole. Kim loved the maypole, her arms were really strong through walking on all fours and she could hang on like a limpet going around the pole. We then headed down to the Malone Road where we visited the Botanic gardens and the Belfast Museum. We were experts on the works of art in that museum! At 2 o'clock we walked over to Wellesley Avenue, where 'our club', the YWCA was situated. There we played table tennis and sang and played the piano. At around 5.30pm we landed home for tea and religiously sat in front of the television to watch Ron Ely as Tarzan followed by the Monkees. We were all tucked up in bed straight after 'The Beverley Hillbillies' as we were so tired by the events of the day. All in all, Mum and Dad played a blinder on Saturdays, seven kids all fully occupied from 10 o'clock in the morning till bedtime!

The YWCA held an annual holiday for the members. A weekend away was arranged either to Bangor or Newcastle. All five girls in our family went away for the planned weekend. Mum and Dad knew we were able to look after Kim and her daily routine. Elizabeth was a master at putting Kim's limbs on. Between the both of them, they had it down to a fine art. In reality, it took Kim no longer than anyone else to get ready in the morning. The time had long since passed when Kim would complain that she wanted to leave her limbs off, she knew she could go nowhere with the rest of us if we had to carry her. Even so, if Kim's limbs became sore around her hips or back as they often did, Elizabeth would take them off for a while. We were all well used to carrying Kim around 'piggy back' style if she was tired.

Thin cotton socks were worn by Kim to stop the leather casts from chafting the tops of her legs. Even with the socks on, she was often red raw in the evening when her limbs came off. The limbs worn most often were made from metal and leather. Leather casts made to fit the shape of Kim's legs, had long extra strong laces to fasten them around her legs. The whole lace had to be undone every night and redone again in the morning. The laces were the longest we had ever seen, and were specially made to lace up the leather bootees. Once the casts were on, the metal frame of the limbs were laid against the chair in front of Kim and she put her legs into the metal leg-casts. These consisted of two metal legs covered in pink 'skin-coloured' vinyl, joined together with two chrome bars, one on the outside of each leg. The chrome bars joined a very strong leather covered metal belt which was buckled around Kim's waist.

Over the years there were many variations, some good, some not so good but the basic design was similar throughout. One major 'improvement' was developed by the technicians at Musgrave Park Hospital. When Kim walked, she was very 'stiff' looking. To make her legs go forward, she had to use her shoulders and hips to swing her left leg and then her right. As the limbs were made from metal, the legs were completely straight as Kim walked. One cruel remark typical, in response to seeing Kim walk in with her limbs,

"Look! Here comes Frankenstein's daughter!"

One person who uttered these words in earshot of Elizabeth and Joan, was sorry she had bothered when they both rallied to Kim's defence and chased her off with a 'flea' in her ear to say the least!

To redress the problem, the technicians devised a 'hinge' down each side of the limbs, attached to the chrome bar. When pulled up, it 'clicked' and released the kneecap of each leg creating a bent leg movement. Kim hated it! She practically had to learn to walk all over again, and every time she took a step a loud 'clunk' accompanied her every move! She refused to use the hinges leg and for a while kept the bar firmly in the lock position.

Alex, our eldest brother, was working in England by this stage, and when he came home, he encouraged Kim to use the hinge.

"If you can walk the length of the hall by the time I go back to England, I will give you a pound note!" he teased.

Immediately Kim started to use the hinge. She idolised her big brother, and of course the pound was extremely enticing too! Each day she walked a little further, falling over and hauling herself up promising she would make the length of the hall next day.

We often heard Kim mocking herself saying,

"Kerplunk! Kerplunk!" as she walked with the hinge released.

But she was determined to relieve Alex of his much advertised pound note before he returned to England! Finally the day arrived, Alex was due to leave, and we all stood around Kim shouting words of encouragement, (and some heckling was heard in the back)

"Come on Kim, you can do it!" we yelled.

Kim stood, smiling ear to ear, she stuck her tongue out as Trevor yelled,

"Easy! Easy!"

The moment arrived. Looking just like one of the gunfighters from the O.K. Corral, Kim released the hinges one by one.

"CLUNK! CLUNK!"

As she steadied herself, she looked at Alex.

"You'd better have a pound for me, show me the money!" she demanded with a smirk.

Alex dipped into his trouser pocket and extracted a crisp pound note. He flourished the note tantalisingly above his head then swept the note under Kim's nose just to let her have a brief whiff of the prize. We giggled at the spectacle and the atmosphere was electric. It was one of those moments when the world seemed to be perfect!

"Well, here goes!" Kim declared.

She steadied herself again and set off full of confidence. We cheered her on to one end of the hall, she turned and cheekily walked tall and strong to the other end! She was making sure there was no misunderstanding about the deal! Alex threw his arms around Kim and cheerfully handed over the 'prize'.

'Next time I come home, I expect to see you running down the hall with your legs bent!" he announced.

"No chance" Kim answered back, "The hinges will have rusted over by then, I'm never using them again! I only did it for the pound!" she giggled. "Thanks Alex!"

Kim never did use the hinges again, she simply couldn't get used to the noise and although it made her look slightly less 'robot-like', the disadvantage of the percussion accompaniment could never outweigh the confidence she already had using her 'basic' limbs. The only advantage we could see was cosmetic, she looked better, but it felt wrong to Kim, and that was what was important.

Shoes to fit the feet on the limbs were always a problem. Not least when Kim became fashion-conscious. To facilitate the balance of the feet, completely flat shoes were necessary. The heel was only one and a half inches high, but Mum knew it would be a problem for the technicians. Kim refused to have any more flat shoes, all her friends were wearing shoes with heels. Mum tried her best to persuade Kim, but to no avail.

CHAPTER SEVEN

'Trusting' parents

On her next visit to the limb-fitting centre at Musgrave, Kim proudly showed off her new shoes.

"I'm sorry Kim, there is no way I can allow you to wear these shoes with your limbs, you would fall over constantly" said the technician sympathetically.

Kim looked disappointed. The friendly technician looked at Kim and said,

"I'm sorry Kim, it is impossible to make your shoes fit your limbs, however ... if you leave me those lovely new shoes, I'll do my best to make your new limbs fit your shoes!"

"Brilliant!" Kim beamed. Victory!

"Better than that" the technician said, "If your boyfriend is 6 feet tall, I can make you 6 feet tall too if you want!"

"Really? I'll have to think about that!" Kim said cheekily.

Kim usually had one pair of limbs made each year, if she had a spurt of growth, adjustments could sometimes be made temporarily.

However, on one occasion she gave the technicians a tricky problem!

The snow was lying heavily as we looked out from our bedroom window.

"Yippee! Snow, loads of snow!" Kim whooped.

Sure enough, there it was, the heaviest snow in years! We dressed quickly ready to go out in the snow. Mum wouldn't let us go out as the snow was already melting and we only had one pair of shoes each. We needed to keep them dry for school. When it was wet, we usually had bread-wrappers tied around our shoes to keep us dry, but playing in the snow meant we would be soaked through before school. Kim pleaded to be allowed out in the snow.

"Please, please let me go out and build a snowman Mummy" she said.

"You'll ruin your shoes" Mum answered.

"I can take my shoes off, my feet can't get wet!" Kim said triumphantly.

Mum relented, and out Kim went, accompanied by Trevor, Elizabeth, Joan and myself. We all had our bread-bags tied over our shoes, and were well warned to stay dry. Unfortunately, when Kim came back in, the vinyl covered feet of her limbs looked the worse for wear, the vinyl was hanging off and they were soaked through! The feet had swollen with the water and Kim's shoes wouldn't fit! Mum nearly had a fit!

Kim had several operations to change the shape of her legs. Once, the main ligament at the back of her knee was cut to allow her leg to 'drop' so releasing the sharp bend in her thigh. Another operation removed one finger and graft it to form a thumb on her hand. Kim took all her visits to the hospital in her stride. Mum and Dad had to take Kim on frequent visits to London where specialist doctors monitored her progress. There, the doctors would carry out various tests to determine what steps, if any, could be taken to help the motability of the children. By the age of eight, some of the children had abandoned their limbs refusing to be encumbered with the heavy uncomfortable straps and metal rods. As Kim had always been encouraged to wear hers, she thought nothing of it.

The parents had become a force to be reckoned with. The hospital visits were not the only place where their paths crossed. They were meeting regularly once a month. The committee had raised money over the previous years while hiring solicitors to fight their cases. Money collected was used to pay air-fares for some of the more prominent parents who had taken on the role of campaigners. Dad had visited London and consulted with solicitors alongside other fathers and mothers.

Various social occasions were regularly organised for the families of all the children. At Christmas, a party was held and was well organised. Each child received a gift from 'Wilfred Pickles' a well known television personality at the time. A local chemist, Tom Eakin, organised a boating trip for all the children. He was a member of a boating club near the Ards peninsula and his fellow members joined forces to take every family on a memorable trip.

The Society for the aid of Thalidomide Children was also donating funds towards the expenses incurred by parents daily. The distribution company DISTILLERS was still showing no sign of accepting any responsibility. The Government had not even undertaken a public inquiry. For a long time it looked as if no headway was being made on behalf of their children. Many parents despaired of ever getting any settlement. It looked as if going to court was the only solution.

The prospect of a court case claiming personal injuries was daunting. Most of the parents had never seen the inside of a court, let alone fighting a huge company with what was, after all a very difficult case to prove.

When Dad went through a period of unemployment, he became more involved in the campaign. He made several visits to London on behalf of the parents. Dad was a strong character, and although not well versed in matters of law and litigation, he knew he had right on his side and campaigned vigorously for the rights of all parents. One after another, the parents came up against delays. 62 sets of parents issued writs on behalf of their children.

Counsellors for the parents warned them that there was no precedent for such a claim for an unborn child. They advised the parents to go for a settlement instead. DISTILLERS agreed to a settlement but only if the parents withdrew all claims of negligence from the company. They would admit nothing, but offered to pay only 40% of what they estimated a court would award, if the company was found to be liable. Another stipulation was that each and all of the 62 sets of parents had to agree unreservedly. If one of the 62 declined, the offer would be revoked. The pressure was intolerable, some faced angry reactions from parents who were not in a position to refuse any cash incentive, however small. In a House of Commons debate Barbara Castle declared that some parents who disapproved of the settlement had been threatened with having their legal-aid withdrawn. This would make it impossible for these parents to claim anything! Although this may have been speculation, some parents had no doubt been led to believe it. The solicitors advised acceptance. Meetings were held where parents had to vote by a show of hands, putting even more pressure on individuals to accept or 'spoil' it for everyone else. One parent, David Mason, later wrote:

'I did not really relish joining argument against experienced counsel. I could feel the mood of acceptance in the hall, and I realised I could probably do nothing to change it. And I didn't fancy being booed or maybe lynched.'

Mason estimated that the campaign on behalf of his daughter had cost him over £100,000 in losses. He was able to fight on for justice but how many others could do the same? Most people were already financially burdened and could not go on any longer.

The settlement was also being offered with other strings attached. If everyone agreed, no lump sum would be guaranteed, anything agreed was to be kept confidential. Also, they offered to consider making provision for the other children if all parents without exception agreed to their terms. The 'blackmail' worked, the pressurised and battle-weary parents agreed. Ten years of wrangling had taken its toll. For most parents it seemed 'all or nothing' they couldn't take the gamble. They needed money now.

Unable to agree a settlement figure, two representative cases were decided by the court. One 'middle category injured party' was awarded £32,000, minus the agreed 60% leaving a settlement of

£13,040. Another 'serious injured party' was awarded £20,800. Among the 62 awards, £16,129 was the average. The total settlement was almost £1,000,000. The award was made on the assumption that inflation would cancel out any interest. The agreement was made in July 1969.

In November 1971, a 'charitable trust fund' was proposed by DISTILLERS to take care of the remaining Thalidomide children, £3,250,000 would be paid by instalments over a period of 10 years. On average, each child would receive £8,500. Parents were incensed at the company who they considered responsible for their children's disabilities offering to set up a 'charity'. They refused.

In June 1972 a new offer was proposed. Cash of £2,900,000 or the previous proposal, providing a 'substantial majority' of the parents agreed. Again it was unacceptable. A very high profile publicity campaign was set in motion. Newspapers again took an interest in the plight of the children. DISTILLERS profits had fallen by £8,000,000. They offered £5,000,000 broken down, it would average only 65% of the settlement awarded to the 62 original claimants. Jack Ashley said in a Common's debate:

Distillers were acting as 'Scrooge in the guise of Santa Claus'.

After pressure from all over, including shareholders with DISTILLERS various companies, an offer of £20,000,000 was made. A 2-way choice was offered. (1) £5,000,000 paid immediately and £1,500,000 paid annually for 10 years into a trust fund. OR £2,000,000 paid into a trust fund every year for 10 years. An immediate cash sum of £5,000 would be made to each parent. A payment of £20,000 would be available for administration of the trust for 10 years plus 'reasonable expenses for the legal bills'.

In April 1973, an improved offer was agreed. Immediate cash of £6,000,000 7 years of £2,000,000 the parents offer of £5,000 was still part of the offer. The end result would be £54,000 each child, a vast difference on the £7,500 originally proposed, only 5 couples had held out, now it was at last paying off.

Mum and Dad were one of the original 62 parents. The final settlement was a Trust Fund to help pay for the children's needs throughout their lifetime. So all Thalidomide children would benefit from the trust set up to make provision for them.

Almost a year after the settlement had been agreed, only £150 had been issued to each child, it had been fifteen years since the first child had been born. Also the parents believed the payments would be tax exempt, in the end, they were not!

David Mason, still a very active campaigner put forward a modification for the trust fund. He suggested the fund was applied to the children on a scale dependent on the degree of their disability. He wanted the £6,000,000 paid immediately followed by 80-90% to be paid to the children when they reached their 18th birthday. He then proposed that the remaining 10-20% be held in an 'emergency' fund until the full effects of Thalidomide became known, possibly in 15-20 years time. He felt a survey should be undertaken so as to fully understand the needs of the various children and their disabilities and their implications on the day to day life of each child. His final proposal called for a medical panel to assess the disabilities instead of lawyers.

In May 1973, parents had a meeting and voted to accept the DISTILLER'S offer. Mason decided to end his campaign on the understanding that a panel would assess the disabilities as he had proposed. Another complication which would have a definite effect on the amount of money available to each child was what became known as the 'X' and 'Y' list.

The 'X' list were the children accepted by DISTILLERS as 'Thalidomide', there were 340 on the list. The 'Y' list consisted of 116 children not yet accepted as genuine Thalidomide victims. In July 1973, 433 children were accepted by DISTILLERS as the High Court was satisfied their mothers' had taken Thalidomide in the form of Distaval. The change from the 'Y' list to the 'X' list happened gradually and is still going on at the time of writing. Years of assessments followed, albeit no longer in the public eye. The fund was held back from making investments due to several legal and tax problems. The Government refused to make any provision for tax relief on the funds payments to children, except to offer £5,000,000 to offset taxation, and exemption on alterations to homes or buying houses.

Kim's final settlement figure was £19,500, while Mum and Dad received a total of £1,900 each.

Once up and running, the trust set about meeting the varied needs of the children. Kim was getting through about two dresses a week, and the cotton socks she wore under her leather bootees to cushion the chafing on her legs only lasted once or twice before holes appeared in them. Up until now, Mum had struggled to make do and mend kim's clothing, with patches in her dresses and stitching the socks. The mended areas caused irritation as they rubbed against her skin. With 7 children all growing at various stages, it was proving expensive. Every spare penny had to go on new clothing for Kim, Mum decided to write to the trust.

Mum sat down and composed a letter to the trustees in charge of the Thalidomide trust fund. She wasn't sure how to make her request, but Kim needed regular new socks and dresses, she had to at least ask! She received a letter to say the 3 trustees would be in Belfast to meet with 2 other sets of parents. The letter gave a date for an appointment and the meeting was to take place in the Stormont Hotel.

Mum and Dad arrived at the Hotel unsure what to expect. The 3 trustees sat opposite Mum and Dad and the other parents and began discussing the needs of each family. Mum felt very uncomfortable, she felt like a beggar. The questions asked, seemed quite personal and the atmosphere was making Mum feel very inferior. When the trustees said they were staying in the Hotel while they assessed each family, Mum began to feel very angry. She thought of the expensive hotel, the air fares for 3 people and the patronising attitude when they had asked for 'proof' of expenses. Here they were sitting in a luxury hotel ordering food and drink on an all expenses paid trip and all Mum had asked for was £5 per week to buy socks and a dress for Kim!

Mum stood up and told the trustees how annoyed she was at their attitude to all the parents.

"You're sitting here ordering coffee and scones which cost more than I'm asking to clothe my daughter, and heaven knows how much it cost to send 3 of you over here to stay in this hotel! I suppose the cost will come out of the children's money!" Mum said exasperated.

Dad sat with his mouth open. He had never seen Mum like that before, it was not in her nature to be so outspoken and he knew she must have been really upset to have been so forceful. The trustees mumbled while Mum and Dad left, unsure of how things would ever work out. It has been a long hard battle with the courts and DIS-TILLERS, Mum felt drained, if they couldn't even allow money for clothes Kim badly needed, what was it all about.

After a while, a letter arrived from the Trust to say an account had been opened in Marks & Spencer in Kim's name. Mum could buy clothing in the store up to the value of £120 per year. Mum was glad that at least they had made some headway towards helping Kim.

When Mum and I called in to Marks & Spencer to buy Kim some new clothes, she wasn't too sure what the procedure would be regarding the account. She called at the information counter to enquire. The assistant gave Mum a form to fill out and explained that whatever Mum bought would have to be brought back to the counter and signed for.

Mum and I chose a new dress for Kim and four pairs of socks. As advised, she brought the items over to the counter. The assistant was not sure how to deal with the account so she began a humiliating to-ing and fro-ing to find out what to do with this 'special needs' account. By the time things were organised, a queue had formed behind Mum, and everyone in the queue seemed to have heard all about the 'account'. Mum couldn't wait to get out of the shop, she hadn't expected such a fuss, we hurried off to catch the next bus home.

"Why will the trust not let you have some real money to buy clothes for Kim, then you could go into any shop you wanted?" I asked.

"I wish I knew, Beatrice, I suppose they want to make sure the money is spent on Kim" she answered.

I remember feeling so sorry for Mum that day, she had such an ordeal in the shop. Mum was always quite easily embarrassed.

From then on, anything Kim needed, had to be applied for either by letter or phone call. The trustees would decide whether the request merited a payment and a cheque was sent off. An estimate or bill had to be supplied for whatever purchase was made.

With the cash Mum and Dad received from the settlement, Dad bought a second-hand car, and a second-hand caravan. The caravan was situated in our favourite seaside resort Millisle, on the Ards peninsula. Mum bought new furniture and carpets for the house, with 7 kids running about we needed new things badly!

We spent most weekends at Millisle, we made a tree swing over a stream, and Trevor, Kim, Joan, Elizabeth and myself spent many happy hours on that swing!

CHAPTER EIGHT

Kim & Co legs it!

The 'Troubles' were at their peak in the early 70's and Mum and Dad wanted us to be able to play out as much as possible. Millisle was a quiet seaside village which came alive every July and August with holidaymakers. As soon as we had all arrived home from school on Fridays, it was 'all systems go' to get ready for the caravan. We all piled into the car, and sang along to our favourite songs during the journey.

One Sunday evening, on the way back home from the caravan, our car was stopped at a checkpoint. We were all asleep in the back seat, lying against each other 'al-la-broken-necks'. Kim was lying with her head on my lap minus her limbs, they were in the boot of the car.

"Evening sir" said the young soldier, in an English accent. "Where are you coming from?"

"Millisle" Dad answered.

The soldier was talking on his radio confirming our car registration when he asked Dad.

"Would you mind stepping out of the car and opening your boot please sir?"

"Certainly son" Dad replied as he opened the car door.

As Dad opened the boot, the young soldier turned white as he spotted the pair of legs lying lifeless. Dad knew what he was thinking, and devilishly allowed him a moment to watch the young soldier start to panic.

"I'm going to have to ask you to s-stay here w-while I inform my s-superior" he stammered.

"It's okay, son, they're my daughter's artificial legs, see?" Dad said as he knocked on the steel leg for sound effect.

The soldier was relieved, the panic was over! During the 'Troubles' our car was stopped many times with Kim's legs either lying in the back seat or the boot, it was fun to see people's reaction, though a bit naughty to let them believe they'd happened upon something more sinister!

One Saturday, Mum and Dad had arranged to take Elizabeth, Joan and Kim to see 'the Luv Bug' 'Herbie Goes Bananas' in the Classic Cinema in Great Victoria Street, Belfast. They were just getting ready to leave when a friend of Dad's phoned to ask for a lift to the airport, he was desperate, his car had broken down. Rather than disappoint the girls, Dad asked Trevor if he would accompany them to the cinema and look after them. Mum and Dad would go to the airport and collect everyone on the way back.

When they arrived at the cinema the queue stretched all the way down the street from the main entrance. Everyone was really excited about seeing Herbie, at the time the 'Herbie' films were the most popular films in the cinema.

Trevor settled everyone into their seats and the film started. The chase had hardly begun when an announcement came over asking everyone to leave the cinema by the nearest exit, there was a bomb scare! Panic and pandemonium ensued, Kim had to be carried by Trevor, people were pushing and shouting, Elizabeth and Joan were together but couldn't see Trevor or Kim!

Everyone piled out onto the street screaming and calling out for friends. Trevor, still carrying Kim called out.

"Joan! Elizabeth! Joa-a-nn! Eliz-a-abeth!"

They heard his voice and eventually found each other, but they were upset and didn't know what to do. Trevor looked over towards 'The Institute' school. The wall was low, but if they lay on the grass behind the wall, at least they would have some protection if the bomb went off!

"Come on! Grab a leg each and we'll carry Kim, hurry up!"

They both grabbed a leg each while Trevor carried Kim holding her under her arms. They ran for the wall and lay down on the grass behind the dense brickwork. By the time they lay down, the girls were crying. Joan had been caught in a bomb scare once before while she was shopping in Belfast with me. We had run around in circles because everywhere we ran there had been roads blocked, it was really scary, but we eventually escaped unhurt. Trevor tried to calm everyone down.

"It's okay, we'll be home soon, I promise" he said.

"BOO!O!M!!!!!"

The whole area around them shook and swayed, the sound was deafening! All around people were screaming and crying. Trevor held back his tears, he had to look after the girls. Joan screamed,

"I'm bleeding!"

Joan's leg was covered in blood, a piece of flying glass had lodged in her leg, it wasn't serious, but she was frightened at the sight of blood. When she had calmed down, and felt alright, Trevor helped Kim up, and they walked towards Sandy Row to find Frances. She worked in a shoe shop not far from there, near the cinema.

Trevor sent Elizabeth into the shop to ask Frances for money to pay their bus fares. Frances insisted on coming outside to make sure they were safe and sound.

"Are you all okay?" she asked, "I'll leave work early and take you all home" she said.

"It's okay, we won't be long until we're home" Trevor said.

She gave Trevor the money for the bus home. The town was in uproar, the buses were running here, there and everywhere! People only wanted one thing! To get out of town as soon as possible! Eventually Trevor spotted a bus which would take them most of the way home, at least they would be out of town! They would just have to walk the rest!

The bus left them at the Malone Road, about 2 miles from home. The only way home was down a narrow road called Shaw's Bridge. It was beginning to get dark and there were no lights along the road, so they had to be careful.

"Get on my back!" Trevor told Kim. "I'll carry you."

"No, I'm walking, it's too far to carry me, I'll be okay" Kim insisted.

Mum and Dad arrived into town to find roads blocked and police and army everywhere. They were frantic with worry.

"What's going on?" Dad asked as he leaned out of the car window.

"There's been a bomb! In the Classic Cinema! A crowd of disabled children were in the cinema, it was terrible!" gasped the onlooker.

"O my God Alex, my babies!" Mum cried. "Please God let them be alright!"

Tears filled her eyes as they drove slowly through the traffic jam, edging slowly towards Great Victoria Street.

"Don't worry love, they'll be okay, Trevor will look after them" Dad assured her.

"We should have been with them!" Mum shouted.

"If anything has happened to them I'll never forgive myself!" Mum sobbed.

Dad was sick with worry, but kept calm for Mum's sake. He stopped the car, got out, and spoke to a police officer nearby. Mum watched as the policeman pointed and gestured towards 'The Institute', she could feel the panic grip her as Gad got back into the car.

"What? What's happening? Where are the kids?" she cried.

"Calm down now, the policeman said someone reported seeing disabled children lying down behind the wall at the Institute, but there's no-one there now, maybe Trevor had the sense to get a taxi home" Dad explained.

"Find a phone! See if they're home!" Mum insisted ...

Dad drove slowly through the traffic until they found a phone box. He dialled the number with Mum holding her ear to the outside earpiece.

"Lift the phone!" Mum said hopefully.

The phone rang and rang, no-one answered. Mum and Dad decided to drive home immediately, there was nothing else they could do. They arrived home to an empty house, where they waited anxiously for any news.

Meanwhile, Trevor carried Kim on his back as Elizabeth and Joan followed behind him in single file holding on to each others' coats. Kim kept insisting she could walk, but Trevor wouldn't hear of it. He knew her legs were usually red raw by evening time, and if she walked she would be in agony by the time she got home.

Tired and hungry, they arrive home around an hour and a half after getting off the bus! They had hardly knocked the front door, when Mum opened it, her face streaming with tears of relief. There were hugs and kisses all round, and after a warm bath, we had a laugh when we heard about Kim being carried across the street by Elizabeth and Joan holding a leg each! On the news later that night, we found out that the bomb had actually been in a hotel right next door to the cinema.

"When can we go back to see Herbie?" Kim asked later!

Joan had her wound dressed and was none the worse for wear, and Trevor got all the praise for keeping his head under pressure! But every time we thought about Kim being carried like a 'wounded soldier' or the onlooker telling Dad about the 'crowd of disabled children' we had to laugh! It was a day none of us would forget, thankfully no-one was badly hurt.

Many bombs went off in Belfast with tragic results, sometimes the dead and wounded numbered double figures, we lived with it every day in Northern Ireland during the height of 'the troubles' in the early seventies. On that particular day our family survived, others didn't.

Because of the situation in Northern Ireland, the city of Belfast became like Fort Knox. No-one could enter the city perimeter without being searched first. Huge security gates stood at every main entrance surrounding the city centre. Security guards searched bags and parcels, and men and women were 'fleeced' down by male and female guards.

When I pushed Kim in her wheelchair, through the gates, the security guards always checked down each side of the chair for incendiary devices. No-one was exempt, as devices had even been smuggled in beside babies as they lay in their prams!

When Kim was 'fleeced', the security guards sometimes caught their fingers or knuckles on the metal bars of her limbs, ouch! Invariably, they were embarrassed and apologised to Kim, even though they were usually the injured party!

When Kim was ten, the doctors asked her to consider having her legs amputated. Kim didn't like the idea but the doctors explained how much more successful her artificial limbs would be, and said her walking in general would improve. As she was still not sold on the idea, the date was set for an operation, it was left 'open' which operation they would finally perform.

When the day arrived, Kim was admitted to the surgical ward. She had decided not to go for amputation, instead she would have the large ligament behind her knee cut and lengthened so her foot would turn outwards. It was a major operation, and meant a long stay in hospital during which Kim made many friends.

One young girl in particular became a good friend. Her name was Ruth, she came from Omagh, which was a long way from the hospital. In those days cars were not as common so it was difficult for her parents to visit as often as they would have liked to. Kim and Ruth talked and played and were really good company for each other.

Ruth had both her legs amputated and was in a bad state, both girls had to have physiotherapy, it was hard work, but together they helped each other. Kim had a happy-go-lucky attitude and plenty of visitors, we lived quite near and there was always one of us free to visit! The nurses were pleased at Ruth's progress since Kim became her friend and when it came time for Kim to leave the hospital there were tears all round!

Both girls were sad to say good-bye, but Kim promised she would visit as soon as she could. A couple of weeks later, Kim asked if Mum and Dad would take her to visit Ruth, she was concerned about her and wanted to see if she was getting any better and doing her exercises.

When Kim arrived, she walked straight over to Ruth and asked her, how she was keeping. Ruth appeared a little wary of Kim for a moment or two, until she suddenly realised who Kim was! She couldn't believe Kim was walking! She had only ever seen Kim without her artificial limbs. Ruth started to cry, she seemed very upset. Kim asked,

"What's wrong Ruth, what's happened?"

"I'm just crying because I thought I would always be in a wheelchair, and I'd never be able to walk again! Now I see you walking, I can hardly believe it's really you! I want to be just like you! Do you think I could have limbs just like yours?" Ruth asked, the tears drying on her cheeks.

"I'm sure you can, you can learn to walk again! I promise!" Kim enthused.

They talked for a while until Kim had to leave, they promised to keep in touch. Unfortunately, as often happens, the two girls lost touch, but Kim never forgot Ruth. I'm sure Kim inspired Ruth to learn to walk again, she had a positive effect on everyone she met.

When Kim was finally fit enough to return to school, she had a lot of catching up to do. An engineer had developed a small 'dodgem' type car for Kim to get around in while she was recovering. One little switch controlled the forward, back, left turn and right turn. Kim became a fine little driver, and would race after us, when we crossed her path! We called her Penelope Pitstop, and she would drive around and around the house until the battery ran out!

On school sports day, Kim suggested to her teacher that she could drive around the obstacle course in her car and show the course to the participants. The teacher thought it was a novel idea, and of course it meant Kim could participate in sports day in spite of her still weakened leg. Kim rode around the course pointing out each obstacle as the teacher called out each one over the megaphone! Kim was in her glory!

We had moved to a new bungalow, the trustees and solicitors had advised parents to invest the children's money in property. We moved into a bungalow, mainly to make life easier on Kim, but Mum and Dad should have known better!

The attic room was adapted as an extra bedroom, Elizabeth, Joan and Kim wanted to have the attic room! As usual, Kim was adamant she wanted to sleep in that room and wouldn't hear of taking another room!

The only access to the room was a metal ladder which was pulled down from the trap-door via a hooked pole, Kim was soon an expert at unhooking and pulling the pole down to the ground floor. The three girls called a meeting with Mum and Dad.

"We want to decorate our room the way WE want it!" they declared.

Dad started to reason them out of it, but was outnumbered and finally gave in. They chose a ghastly purple paint (popular in the early seventies) and burnt orange. (I know, I know, the mind boggles!) The main colour was burnt orange but they had a use for the deep purple ... footprints on the ceiling! Elizabeth and Joan dipped their feet in the paint and lay on their backs, legs in the air, and pressed their footprints onto the low ceiling. Kim however, hard as she tried, couldn't make an impression, as her feet were turned in, the only impression was the mark of her ankle bone! Elizabeth had an idea, she lifted Kim while Joan took Kim's foot and turned it in towards the ceiling.

"OW! I'm not made of Plasticine!" Kim groaned.

Elizabeth had another idea, she put her curled up fist into the paint from the little finger to the wrist, and pressed a 'print' on the ceiling. She then put her fingertips into the paint and 'dotted' Kim's footprint! Kim was delighted, and it was years before she admitted the footprints were not made by her own feet! The girls' bedroom was like a dungeon, but it was their private space, and they made the most of it! Kim was especially fond of that bedroom as she was the only one who didn't bump her head periodically on the low ceiling!

The only special alterations made to the bungalow were the light switches, they were lowered about 6 inches to allow Kim to reach them, Other than that, nothing else was different. Kim disliked having anything done especially for her. In fact she considered anything likely to cause her a problem as a challenge. Her common-sense matter-of-fact attitude to those challenges often amazed us all.

As Kim was fast becoming a young lady, she wanted a pair of jeans. The rest of us girls wore them every day, and when Mum bought her a pair, it took three of us to get the jeans over her limbs. But it was worth it just to see the look on her face as she looked at her reflection in the full length mirror! She was really pleased at her figure in the jeans. As soon as it was possible, the technicians at Musgrave Park set about making her limbs a little more 'stream-lined' so she could wear trousers and jeans of course!

Up until then, Kim's leather encased legs simply dangled in full view with the lower part of her limbs shaped like a leg from the 'knee to the foot'. The technicians designed a full length shaped leg to encase the leather 'boots' which Kim wore over her own legs. By making the 'thigh' thick enough, the steel leg completely covered the leather boot, so the leg appeared to be less 'lumpy'.

Kim had to attend classes at Musgrave for a brief period to learn how to walk with the extra weight of the new limbs. While at one class, she watched a man in his early 30's trying in vain to climb stairs with artificial legs. The man became more and more agitated as each time he failed to swing one leg up one step. Kim walked over to him;

"You'll never get up those stairs doing it like that, you're trying to get up the way you did when you had your own legs! Limbs are different, completely different. Watch and I'll show you how to do it" she said.

Kim moved over to the short staircase which was specially made for climbing practice, and put both her hands on the bannister. As she stepped sideways up each step, the man watched in amaze-ment as Kim went to the top and back down again;

"See, you go sideways like a crab, you have a go, go on! You can do it. If a kid like me can do it so can you!" she encouraged him.

As he shook his head, his face broke into a wonderful mischie-vous smile.

"Yes! If a little girl like you can do it then I certainly can!" he announced.

He put his hand on the rail just as Kim had, and moved up the stairs smiling the whole way up and down again, with vigorous encouragement from Kim. When he finished he smiled at Kim and took a bow. Immediately Kim curtsied and everyone laughed. Later as Mum and Kim talked to the man, they discovered he had been a victim of the Abercorn bomb disaster in Belfast. He had lost both of his legs, and was learning to walk with artificial limbs. He had been frustrated trying to get up stairs, and was grateful to Kim for showing him how! In the carpark, as they said goodbye, Kim remarked how nice the man's car was and how she would love to drive someday.

"Don't ever let them put you in one of those three wheeled disabled cars, you're much too beautiful!" he said as he drove away.

The following visit, Kim met another victim of the Abercorn bomb. She was a woman in her forties who had also lost both her legs, and had a large part of her arm missing. She was using the 'black-rockers' as Kim called them. They were structured to help amputees learn to balance before any limbs were designed for them. The 'legs' consisted of two metal bars with black blocks on the end instead of feet.

The woman looked very nervous as she stood in the middle of the parallel bars (which were on either side of her so she could hold onto them while she found her balance). As the woman began to walk forward, Kim noticed she also had two walking sticks which she seemed reluctant to put down.

"Can you walk without the walking sticks?" Kim asked.

"No I can't" she replied.

Each time the woman tried, Kim kept encouraging her to put the walking sticks away. Eventually she put them down and held on to the parallel bars for balance.

"Leave go of the bars, you can do it, come on!"

Spurred on by Kim's enthusiasm, the woman let go of the parallel bars and walked two complete lengths of the bars unaided! By the end of the two-week session, Kim and the woman had become good friends.

Because of the terrorism in Northern Ireland a lot of able-bodied people were tragically plunged into a world they didn't know, their limbs were torn off in explosions and they had to learn to walk all over again. It was heart breaking, but Kim considered herself luckier than most of the people learning to walk at Musgrave. She reckoned she'd never had legs and so knew nothing different, to have legs and lose them, was a lot worse.

I like to think that Kim helping that man to climb the stairs and the woman to feel confident enough to let go of the bars, had a positive effect on their recoveries. It came naturally to her to encourage both of them to walk, she has a gift to inspire people to accept a challenge and overcome it.

I have watched her cast her spell and encapture people with her zest and courage, all of my life. I am proud to be one of her 'big' sisters, but it's best if you read Kim's own story from here on, as things are changing fast at home. Alex has been in the army for a few years now, Frances is working in a local company, Trevor has an apprenticeship as a plumber, and Elizabeth, Joan, Kim and I are still at school. Mum has just started a new job as a civil servant in Stormont, while Dad is driving an HGV for a bottled gas company in Belfast.

The Gentle 'Giant'

In the street where we lived there were lots of games to play
Rounders, if we could pick a team, but someone would always say ...
"I don't want to play with you lot, because you always win"
For our street were very good and the other side were hardly ever in!
To hear the screams and shouts of us, the neighbours would complain,
And say we were never to play outside their door again.

The world outside our street seemed to be a mystery to most of us,
And it was rare to say the least to go on a journey on a bus
So imagine our delight one day when a stranger came to our street,
He was the tallest man we'd ever seen and had such enormous feet!
He called to see my Mum that day, and asked her very politely
If he could possibly take the family out of a picnic for the day.

After a while the word got around about this very generous man,
The children swarmed around him and tried to take his hand.
They knew whoever got there first would be taken for a treat,
To the big house on the hill, the very poshest place to eat!
It was a wonder to behold this very gentle man at play
He seemed to enjoy every moment with us, and he would often say:

"Dear children, you're so wonderful, you make my heart leap with joy"
He became so dear to us, we all loved him, every girl and boy.
At Christmas time he would call for us and take us in his car
To a retirement home in a beautiful park, not very far.
There we would sing carols in our voices so sweet and bright
The elderly peoples' hearts would soar their faces showing pure delight.

Afterwards our gentle friend would take us to his friend
Where we would receive the nicest and most thoughtful presents.
Inside their house was the biggest tree in the world,
At least it had always seemed to be, when I was a little girl.
I had happened to mention one day about the marvellous tree,
The next thing I was invited into their home to look and see!

During summertime was the best, we had so many trips out,
We were at the 'Giant's Ring', Downpatrick and all about.
No matter what we said or did he was kind and understanding
I'd never met anyone so patient, and we kids were so demanding.
On one day in particular he brought a large crowd of young ones
To the big house on the hill for afternoon tea and hot buttered scones.

When decimal coins were first introduced in presentation folders
He called to bring me one of them, and one for Trevor who was older.
His thoughtfulness amazed me time and time again.
He had a different game to play every time he came
Sometimes he would throw a tennis ball high into the sky
And who ever caught it got a sixpence so you really had to try!

So many lovely memories were left to me by this very gentle man
He enriched by childhood and encouraged me to be who I really am.
He praised me for all the little things most people would ignore
When he was around I felt special in a way I'd never felt before.
He had a gift so very rare, a special gift of joy and love
He was man of God you see, he was sent from above
To brighten up the long dull days of all the children in our street
The nicest, most considerable gentle giant you could ever wish to meet!

~ Beatrice Atcheson 1986

CHAPTER NINE

My initiation

When I was eleven I started secondary education. Most of my friends from Braniel Primary School had transferred with me, so I had plenty of people who were used to me. Every 35 minutes the bell would ring and we had to change rooms for another lesson. For the first two weeks my friend, Sandra, carried me upstairs on her back. To go downstairs, I put my arm around her neck and she tucked me under her arm and hauled me downstairs. It was exciting being at the high school, it was very different from primary school and I was really enjoying the variation going from class to class. The only problem was, Sandra and I were always the last two into the class. None of the teachers appeared to mind. When the bell rang, the corridor was like a cattle market, it was every one for themselves!

After two weeks in school, I was really getting into the routine when the headmaster, Mr. Cave, called to see my form teacher. He later informed me that I was to have all my classes in room 7. He explained that as I had to climb so many stairs during the day it was felt I could cope better if all my classes were on ground level. I agreed feeling I had no choice, but inside I was already missing my friends. Each day that passed I felt more and more alienated. I felt I was singled out for preferential treatment and I hated it! For five full days I bit my lip and pretended to be as happy as ever but I eventually reached boiling point.

All my life I had been used to being treated the same way as everyone else, I knew Mr. Cave was trying to help, but I was so unhappy I had to do something about it!

At 3.30 pm on the fifth day of my 'torture', I knocked on the headmaster's door. I was determined to stay calm, but my lip trembled and my eyes filled with tears as I blurted out the whole story about how miserable I had felt all week and how I missed all my friends. Poor Mr. Cave, he hadn't realised how much misery he had caused me and he readily agreed that I should resume my old schedule with one exception. I was to leave five minutes earlier than the rest of the class, to avoid the mad rush at changeover.

"Suits me fine, especially when I had double maths!" I thought.

My friends all rallied round and took it in turns to carry me up and down to each class.

Six months into my first year, I almost ruined my chances of staying at Lisnasharragh school for good! During cookery class, my friend Dawn and I asked to be excused to go to the toilet. As we were washing our hands, I leaned forward to listen near a metal box attached to the wall in the toilet block.

"Can you hear that ticking noise?" I asked Dawn.

"Yeah I can, what is that?" she said.

We listened again and suddenly I shouted, "It's a bomb!"

At the time the troubles in Northern Ireland were pretty bad, and we were told to be alert about anything suspicious. As we rushed to tell our cookery teacher I felt quite pleased with myself. Mr. Armstrong bolted out to next door where the headmistress was teaching. As we watched the two teachers ran up the corridor like two guided missiles! Soon the fire alarm sounded and the whole school was evacuated into the playground of the adjoining school. For two hours the school was taken over by army, fire brigade and police.

Dawn and myself were swamped by television news reporters and police asking us to describe what we had seen and heard, and asking if we were frightened when we realised there was a bomb in our school. Eventually we were all collected by parents and buses, everyone was congratulating me on being a hero, not because of the bomb, but because we all got to leave school early. I was elated, and Dawn and myself were feeling very full of ourselves.

Later in the evening all the family sat patiently waiting for the local news to come on television. Near the end of the programme a brief mention was made about 'a hoax bomb in an east Belfast school'. I was disappointed not to see myself on television, but I went to bed that night feeling pretty smug.

The following day I was summoned to the headmaster's office.

"Probably a pat on the back" I thought to myself as I imagined how I would react to all the praise.

As I entered Mr. Cave looked a little agitated.

"Miss Rodgers!" he thundered, "Get your parents to teach you the facts of life! The ticking noise you and your friend heard yesterday was the ticking of the timer on the sanitary towel incinerator!"

Although he sounded angry I knew he was finding great difficulty keeping his face straight, the amusement in his eyes almost made me burst out laughing myself, but I somehow restrained myself.

"Yes sir, sorry sir," I said as I shrugged my shoulders.

What else could I say? Overnight, the whole school knew who Kim Rodgers was!

From that day on, I was considered 'one of the girls'. A mischief maker! I couldn't have staged a better initiation ceremony if I'd tried!

Another incident was to give everyone a laugh, and only reinforced my reputation as a prankster.

After lunch we were waiting for a teacher to appear. A boy in our class had a club biscuit in his hand.

"Who wants this?" he asked. "I've had enough lunch and can't finish this."

"I'll have it if no one else wants it," I offered.

I unwrapped the biscuit and broke it in two, and gave half to Sandra. We were munching away when the teacher arrived She looked around the desk and lifted the papers as if looking for something.

"Right!" she bellowed, "Who stole my club biscuit?"

Sandra and I froze, mouths still full, crumbs stuck around our lips, there was no escape, we admitted our crime! We were sent to Mr. Meneely, the head teacher (a strict disciplinarian who instilled fear into every pupil who stepped out of line) and given an ultimatum, pay two-and-a-half pence each towards a new chocolate biscuit, or detention. Needless to say the fine was paid!

During my time at Lisnasharragh Secondary school I became particularly fond of one teacher. When I was younger I used to have times when my body would simply seize and I became paralysed.

When this happened, I was totally unable to move and the pain was unbearable. I was never told exactly why it occurred or what could cause it, so I had no control over it. Obviously it was embarrassing when it happened and sometimes it would last for hours.

One day during lunch in the school dinner hall, it happened. There was usually no warning and once it had started, I was helpless. Even the slightest move was excruciating! My friends tried to help but it was useless.

Miss Carnahan, my English teacher, came over to see what was happening. Once she realised how serious it was, she discreetly called two other teachers over to help carry me to the office. As I couldn't move at all, they had to carry me in a very awkward position the whole way down the corridor!

In the office, Miss Carnahan was very sympathetic and understanding, and stayed with me as long as she could. I had been so embarrassed at going into that state in front of my school friends, and I was grateful for her help just at the right moment. When I was finally able to move, I'd been in the office for almost two hours!

In class, Miss Carnahan encouraged me at every opportunity and opened my eyes to books and reading. I've never forgotten her kindness to me, it meant a lot.

CHAPTER TEN

On top of the world

My older brother, Alex, was getting married, he asked Beatrice and myself to be bridesmaids, we were really looking forward to it! The whole family travelled to England for the ceremony. It was a wonderful day!

During the reception, I was asked to sing with the band who were playing. I was excited at the prospect, as I had always wanted to sing in public. I had been a soloist in our school choir, and I loved to sing! I dreamed of being a big star! I wasn't the least bit nervous, and when I finished everyone stood up and cheered! I felt wonderful, a perfect end to a perfect day!

Four months later, I was bridesmaid again, along with my sister Frances. This time it was Beatrice's wedding. There were over 100 guests and again I was asked to sing. I sang the same three songs and again the audience clapped and cheered, this was getting to me, I loved every minute of it.

A man came over to Dad and asked him if he would allow me to sing at a few functions, he would pay me £20 to sing the same three songs! Dad said there was no way his 13 year old daughter would be singing in a club! I was so disappointed, I tried my best to persuade Dad to let me, but he was adamant. By now though, I was totally smitten with the entertainment world, I couldn't get enough of singing in public!

Dad allowed me to sing at charity functions though, and I really enjoyed every minute of it. I loved the idea of contributing in some way to making money for various charities.

When I was 14, Mum and Dad took me to a big charity night in the 'Queen's Inn', Belfast. My name was put to the band to call me up for a song. No matter where I went, I was always called, I never found out whether it was Mum or Dad who kept doing it, but I never refused!

While I was on stage, I took little notice of a woman who was talking earnestly to Mum. When I came back to our table, Mum explained that the woman was a well known cabaret artist in Belfast, she had remarked to Mum how good a voice I had. Mum said she hadn't realised I was her daughter, and had been wondering if my parents would allow me to do a few 'bookings'. She was an old friend of Mum's called Sylvia Pavis. When Sylvia realised Mum was MY Mum, she asked if I could take some bookings. Mum nodded towards Dad, he looked at me as my eyes pleaded with him and said YES!

Within a few days the phone rang, it was Sylvia with three bookings! There were two of them on the same night, but the first one was at 7 o'clock and the second was at 9 o'clock, a short journey across town would soon make both venues possible. I was so excited! I would earn £50 for all three bookings! I was on top of the world!

Once I became known, the bookings came in thick and fast, for two-and-a-half years, I sang my heart out to audiences all over Belfast. Mum always made sure I wasn't out too late, I still had to go to school in the mornings!

My confidence was growing fast. I attended a circus one night, and after the show the ringleader came over to me.

"Well young lady, what did you think of our show?" he asked.

"It was great, but my sister Joan is a better acrobat than your girl!" I boasted.

"Is she indeed?" he said. "Tell you what, you bring your sister here tomorrow after school, and let me have a look at what she can do, if she's as good as you say, I'll give you both a job! Can't say fairer than that!" he finished.

Joan and I arrived at the circus tent and Joan warmed up for her 'audition'. We had talked about it all night, I came up with some different ideas for positions, I had to make sure Joan did a good job after all my boasting!

The ringleader watched as Joan back-flipped and cartwheeled across the floor, she was good! I watched his face for a glimmer of admiration, he liked what he was seeing, I was sure of it.

"BRAVO!" he shouted as he stood up and clapped.

Joan was embarrassed at such a display of appreciation.

The ringleader offered Joan a job in the circus, as a dancing gymnast, she was as pleased as punch. We spent the whole summer travelling all around the Belfast area with the circus having brilliant fun! Joan was paid £10 a week, while I helped out making candy floss, and taking tickets.

Another summer job we had was taking children for donkey rides at the seaside in Millisle, where we had our caravan. Elizabeth and Joan walked the donkeys up and down the beach while I took the money. We were paid peanuts but we did it for the fun!

We once had to stay at a friend's house while Mum and Dad were away at the caravan. Of course, Elizabeth, Joan and I took full advantage of the situation and stayed out later than we would ever have been allowed to at home! When we got back to our friend's house the door was locked!

We found an open window and everyone clambered in, leaving Elizabeth to lift me in last. However, there was no way I could get in through the window with my limbs on. Once I had my backside on the window sill, I proceeded to release the belt holding my limbs on. Just as I released the last lace, the right limb fell to the ground making an awful clatter! As I looked around to see if anyone was about, I spotted a man walking in a distinct zig-zag, much the worse for too much whisky, by the look of him. I ducked down out of view as he looked over towards the noise. He wasn't too long shifting when he spotted the leg lying on the ground! We laughed so much we were caught out by the grown-ups, but it was worth it!

Of course, the fall didn't do the limb any good, It broke the bar. I had to manage with it until Mum could get it repaired at the limb-fitting centre. However, when we phoned Mum the next day at the place where she was staying, to tell her my leg was broken, she had a strange reaction from a woman at the next table to her. Over hearing Mum explain to Dad that my leg was broken and she would have to take me to the hospital 'next week', the woman looked in disgust at Mum and said, "I don't know how you can sit there and eat when your daughter has just broken her leg! What kind of a mother are you?!"

People often get 'the wrong end of the stick', although it would be hard to blame them! Most people read a situation depending on what they consider 'normal'.

On a night out at a youth club with my sisters Joan and Elizabeth, a young fella came over to speak to me. We were all sitting around talking and having a laugh. There was a group of girls around the same age sitting opposite us and for a while I thought they were talking about me, as I noticed one girl giving me a look of absolute disgust! I ignored her for a while, but Elizabeth overheard her.

My attention was drawn to the young man as he moved away, he had been touching my 'leg'! I didn't know how long it had been going on, as I had no way of feeling his hand, but I suddenly realised why the girls were looking at me in such a disapproving way!

"Are you enjoying yourself?" I asked sarcastically.

"Yes, since you asked," he replied cheekily.

"You haven't been feeling my leg! It's an artificial leg!" I laughed.

Elizabeth and Joan fell about laughing, followed shortly afterwards by the group of girls opposite once they realised the situation! The young fella was embarrassed, but I reckoned he deserved it!

I suppose he would have realised earlier if I had the old, cold metal legs, but I now had vinyl covered legs which felt warm and soft, another improvement the technicians at Musgrave Park had made for me! Those legs were always getting me into trouble.

When I was 16 I went away for the weekend with a youth group. The trip was part of a programme designed to bring both communities in Belfast together. A group of protestant and catholic children were chosen to go away to Ardglass for a weekend.

The scheme was organised by the Youth Opportunities Programme. As we talked together I was pleasantly surprised to find that the children from 'the other side' (as we commonly referred to them') were no different to myself! We got on famously together and had a lot in common. Before the first evening was over, we had forgotten about religion and were simply relating as teenagers, and having a laugh!

The dormitories were sparse, but comfortable in a youth hostel. However, in the girl's dormitory the curtains were a little too short for the length of the window. On Saturday night, there was a disturbance outside the window late in the evening. The incident was reported to the police and they arrived promptly. They looked around the outside but on finding nothing, came in to ask us a few questions about what we had seen and heard.

One police officer suddenly seemed to lose interest in what we were saying. He was transfixed on the floor under my bed.

"Alright son, out you get!" he shouted.

We became scared and cowered back against the wall. The other police officers told us to be calm,

"There's nothing to worry about, we'll soon sort this boyo out! This isn't the first time a peeping Tom has been reported, we've got him now!" he assured us.

"This is your last chance! Come out now before I have to pull you out!" the other officer demanded.

As I craned my neck to try to get a better look, the officer moved towards the bed. My heart was thumping at the thought of someone lying under my bed while I was in it!

"That's it!" the officer insisted.

He then kneeled down and yanked the pair of legs under the bed! The expression on his face was unbelievable as he fell back due to the weightlessness of my limbs! When we realised what had happened, we laughed until our sides hurt! Everyone was highly amused and the police officers took it in good spirits too!

As I became older, things changed quite a lot at home. Alex, Frances, Trevor and Beatrice had all married and had homes of their own. I had two little nieces and two nephews! Elizabeth and Joan had gone to live and work in England, so I was the only one left at home. After growing up with four sisters and two brothers for company, it was strange.

I had a lot of friends and I visited my family regularly. I often baby-sat for Beatrice. I was trusted completely with the little ones, I had never handled a new born baby before, but I don't think it ever occurred to Frances or Beatrice that I wouldn't be able to cope. I revelled in the responsibility of looking after my nieces and nephews!

Mum and Dad seemed to be arguing a lot more, I felt sad about all the arguments, but could do nothing about it, everything was changing at home, and I was no longer a little girl. The big bad world loomed ever nearer.

In 1979, I left for a holiday in Canada. Mum and Dad had friends in Toronto, and we planned to stay with them during our visit. They had emigrated from Belfast and had invited us out to their home for a holiday. Mum, Dad and I set off for Toronto, I was really excited!

When we arrived, we were made very welcome and taken out to many 'Irish' clubs where immigrants from Ireland made anyone from Northern Ireland very welcome indeed. On our first visit, I was called up to sing. I sang my three favourite songs and had a standing ovation! I was delighted! As we toured around, I sang in many different clubs, it seemed everywhere I went, they had heard about 'the wee girl from Belfast with the great voice' (as I heard myself described once). I even sang in a couple of hotels in Florida!

During my stay I became good friends with Georgina, Mum's friend's daughter. We really enjoyed ourselves, and when my holiday came to an end, I was sorry to say goodbye. However, I was invited back to stay the following November! Georgina said her Mum had been asked to bring me back to sing around the clubs again!

I was over the moon!

"You won't have to ask me twice!" I said, "I'd love to come back again!"

"We'll take you to see Nashville, promise!" Georgina said.

Nashville! My dream was to go to Nashville. Ever since I had heard Patsy Cline sing I had dreamed of going to see the place where she had begun her career. She was my idol! I had all her records. My mind wandered during the plane ride home, I imagined myself on stage at 'The Grand Ole Opry' singing just the way Patsy Cline had done so many years before. My voice could never compare with hers of course, no one could in my opinion, but just to be there, ... I couldn't wait! Roll on November!

Fate had different plans for me however, I never did make the return journey to Toronto that year.

When my new artificial limbs were being made, the last stage was the making of the feet. Once I had bought the shoes I wanted and given them in to be measured, Mr. Johnson, the technician, then made the feet fit the shoes. You should have seen his face when he saw the shoes I brought in!

"There is no way you can have these shoes Kim, you'll fall every time you take a step!" he insisted.

The shoes had a two-and-a-half inch heel and I was adamant I wanted them! He nearly had a fit! He refused point blank to even consider fitting the new limbs with them for me.

"You simply won't be able to balance properly, I am sorry Kim, but I can't use these shoes."

"You told me I could choose my own shoes and you would make them fit," I pleaded.

"Yes, but there is a big difference, two-and-a-half inches is too high for you to balance, it just can't be done, sorry Kim."

"Then I'll just have to learn to balance again!" I said defiantly.

"You'll fall over and over again!"

"Then I'll just have to pick myself up more often, I want those shoes, pl —easse?" I said pleading with every ounce of charm I could muster.

He shook his head and excused himself saying he would be back shortly. He returned with 'the Big Chief' Mr. Edwards, he had been in charge of most of my limb-making for as long as I could remember. They were both agreed, it would never work, and tried to convince me to choose a 'more sensible' pair of shoes.

"I'm 17 now, I want to be like other girls my age, I want to wear fashionable shoes, I'll learn to walk with heels!" I almost cried.

The two men looked at each other and shrugged their shoulders, they realised they were fighting a losing battle!

Yes!

When I finally tried out my new limbs, it took me no time to adjust my balance, I was so proud of those shoes I could have flown!

In October 1979, just a week after I received my new limbs, I went out to a disco with some friends. As I was walking past the ladies room towards the disco floor, I slipped on some spilled water and fell flat on my face! I hit the floor hard! As I tried to regain my dignity, I felt two strong arms lifting me as if I were a rag doll!

"Are you okay love?" the young man enquired.

"Fine thanks," was all I could mutter as my face turned deep red with embarrassment.

Later in the evening, I was dancing with my friends, having almost forgotten the incident, when I felt a tap on the shoulder. I recognised the young man as the one who had helped me earlier.

"Can I have this dance?" he said.

I couldn't refuse after such a polite request, and we danced for a little while, then sat down and talked for what seemed forever, we got on really well! At the end of the night, he offered me a lift home, I accepted and by the time I arrived home, we had arranged to meet again. I felt a little guilty as I was still seeing someone, but somehow it didn't matter any more.

Over the next few weeks, Clive and I met as often as we could, we were inseparable! After only a month, he proposed and we became engaged on 14th December. We planned to marry the following June when I would be 18. We had an engagement party and invited all our friends, it was a great night!

Mum and Dad were a little concerned about how fast everything was going, but they were glad I was happy. I assured them I knew exactly how I felt and what I was doing, and they seemed content to let me be.

For the next three weeks everything in the world seemed to be perfect, I was in love and engaged to be married, I had a job in an office working for a youth organisation, life was good!

At home, Mum and Dad were still having problems. Dad was drinking more than usual and Mum was upset quite often. It was difficult, but I was happy in my new found relationship and tried not to worry too much about what was going on at home. After all Mum and Dad had arguments all the time, but they always seemed to get over it.

I had recently started taking driving lessons in a specially converted car. The brake and accelerator were replaced by levers on the steering wheel, as my feet couldn't control the pedals. The car was automatic as it would have been impossible to change gears. I really enjoyed the freedom driving gave me.

I was over the moon when my new Ford Escort was delivered already converted for me to drive away! Everything seemed to be going right for me, I could hardly believe how lucky I was! It seemed nothing could spoil my happiness!

CHAPTER ELEVEN

To 'hell' and back

My hand trembled as I picked up the phone to dial the chemist. Within seconds my worst fears were confirmed.

"Congratulations Mrs. Rodgers, your test is positive!"

I replaced the receiver in stunned silence. As reality began to surface. I started to shake with fear. I looked at my eldest sister in horror. I felt the tears fill my eyes as Frances held me in her arms and broke down hysterically. I had never seen her so emotional before! We both knew that the phone call I had just made would change my life forever.

The worst was yet to come. How could I possible tell Mum and Dad? Neither Frances nor I relished the thought of being the bearer of such news. How would they react? What would they say? Eventually, Frances plucked up the courage, and steeled herself as she walked into the kitchen to tell Mum.

Poor Frances, as she was the oldest girl, she always seemed to be the bearer of bad news. Mum took it really hard. In her eyes she seemed to be completely destroyed, she didn't know what to say or how to react. As I watched her in stunned silence, I thought how she must be feeling. Here I was, her 17 year old daughter, engaged but not yet married ... pregnant!

Mum was angry and distraught she screamed in pain and despair. My heart broke for the pain I was causing my mother, I wanted to die at that moment. Mum reached over to me and shook me hard in utter frustration, the pain was clearly etched on her face. Suddenly she composed herself and hugged and squeezed me until I could hardly breathe!

We all cried for a while, but Mum said she would tell Dad at a suitable time, meanwhile, Frances and I stayed out of the way for the time being.

Shortly after he came in from work, both Mum and Dad left to do the weekly shopping. When they returned, Frances and I had left the house, we didn't want to be there when Dad heard the news!

We had decided to stay at a friend's house until Dad had a chance to calm down after hearing the news from Mum. The door knocked, it was Mum, she had told Dad and he seemed calm.

"Your Daddy wants to talk to you Kim, he's very upset, but he wants to see you." Mum said.

"I don't want to go home Mummy, he'll go mad!"

"Your father only wants to talk to you love, I'll take you up home if you want," my friend Alex offered.

I was reluctant to leave my 'sanctuary', but I knew I would have to face Dad sooner or later. He insisted on taking me, but said Mum and Frances would be better staying in his house, so I got into Alex's car and he drove me up to the driveway of our house. He stopped the car and helped me out towards the door. It seemed an eternity before Dad opened the door, and when he did, he looked perfectly calm and reassuring.

"It's okay love, I just want to talk to you," Dad assured me.

"I'll leave you with your Dad Kim, you'll be alright love!"

I looked at Alex, pleading with my eyes for him to stay with me, I knew instinctively that Dad didn't just want to talk but Alex hugged me reassuringly and headed down the driveway towards the car. I stood watching as he drove away, I was reluctant to go inside, I knew Dad's calmness was a front for what he was really feeling.

I could read the disappointment in his eyes, he had hardly had the chance to get used to the fact that his little girl was engaged, but pregnant! My mouth was dry with fear, I was all alone with my Dad and he was so calm I could almost taste his anger.

As I walked into the living room, Dad was over at the large picture windows, as he closed the venetian blinds, first one, and then the other, so cool and collected, I saw the headlights of Alex's car disappear out of view. As Dad turned to face me I knew then for sure the last thing he wanted to do was talk to me! When Dad had vented his anger, he sent me out of the room, it was as if he couldn't stand to look at me.

"Now get into the kitchen and get it cleaned until it's spotless!" he ordered.

I walked into the kitchen, as I leaned over the sink, I felt worse than I ever imagined I could feel. I closed the kitchen door so I could shut myself away from Dad. Just as I did so, I heard the front door open.

"Where is she?" Mum demanded to know.

Mum came into the kitchen in a terrible state, and from the look of pity and disgust on her face when she saw the state of me, I thought she was going to be mad!

"Oh, I'm sorry love, I should never have left you on your own," Mum sobbed.

I hadn't cried at all in the living room, as I was determined not to let Dad know how much he had hurt me, but I was sobbing uncontrollably by the time Mum came in. As I stood washing the dishes, my tears dripping into the dishwater, I must have looked a pitiful sight as the look of pity and disgust on Mum's face turned to anger.

"I'll never forgive him for this, never! How could he do this to you!"

"It's okay Mummy, I'm alright," I lied.

Mum charged into the living room to confront Dad. I heard raised voices as Mum told Dad she knew as soon as I had mentioned the blinds being closed, that he had no intention of 'talking' to me as promised. As the shouting continued, I closed my eyes and ears, I was in terrible pain, but I blocked it out. I resolved there and then to get out and away from Dad and live my own life. No one would ever treat me like that again! I was going to get married as soon as possible and have my baby!

Then next day, in a friend's house I suddenly felt all the pain and distress of the night before, I broke down and cried so much I thought I would die with the weight of it all. As I left her house, my mind 'clicked', I would never think about last night again! It didn't happen!

The next few weeks passed by with a roller-coaster of events and emotions. The wedding was brought forward to March 15th. All the usual preparations had to be made and I was caught up in it all. I agonised over my decision and wondered if I was doing the right thing, everything was happening so fast, my head was in a spin!

On my wedding day I wore white with all the trimmings, it was a wonderful day and many of my family and friends attended. Things had settled down a bit by then and I was beaming with pride as I linked my Dad's arm as he walked me down the aisle.

CHAPTER TWELVE

Baby makes three

After only five days together Clive was sent on a posting to Germany with his regiment. Being a newly-wed, no provision was made for married quarters, so I went to stay with Beatrice and her husband Billy.

I was a little weepy for a while as I missed Clive so much, but I kept myself busy playing with the children and I drove to Belfast to visit Mum and Dad as often as I could.

When I was about four-and-a-half months pregnant, I found it impossible to wear my limbs, I was afraid I might fall over and hurt the baby, so I stopped wearing them altogether. Clive and I wrote almost every day, it was difficult for me on my own, Beatrice was always there if I needed her, but I felt Clive should be there.

I received a letter from the 'Royal Victoria Hospital' in Belfast to see a specialist. When I arrived I was interviewed by a doctor. I found the whole episode upsetting and patronising!

I was unaware what the appointment was actually about, as I was attending my normal antenatal visits. The doctor sat down and proceeded to tell me that I would have a perfect 'normal baby'. As he put it:

"If an able-bodied woman fell over and broke her arm while she was pregnant, it wouldn't mean her baby would be born with a broken arm."

I felt he was insulting my intelligence, he was trying to assure me my baby would be 'normal' but the way he put it really upset me, I wished I had ignored the appointment! I bit my lip and said nothing.

At one of my regular visits to Doctor Ferris, my gynaecologist, he made it clear that because of the size of my pelvis, I would need to have a Caesarean section. The words 'Caesarean section' bounced around my head and horrified me!

He explained that I would need to deliver the baby three weeks earlier than the due date, to be sure there was no chance of me going into labour myself. My baby would be born on 16th September at 9 am!

As the date drew nearer, Clive and I had been writing as much as ever. Clive wanted out of the army, he asked me to get a letter from my doctor outlining my disability and condition to enable him to get a conditional discharge. I wasn't sure what to do for the best but in the end I got the letter and Clive received his discharge from the army. He was home with me by the end of August.

With just two weeks to go before the birth of my baby, my sister Elizabeth gave birth to a baby girl! Ever since I could remember, she had promised if she ever had a baby girl she would name her after me! She fulfilled her promise. By coincidence, my niece Kim was the seventh grandchild, just as I had been the seventh child born to my parents. I felt really honoured to have someone so precious named after me.

The morning arrived. Outwardly I pretended to be my usual happy self, but inwardly I was terrified. The whole idea of operating tables and anaesthetic and hospital beds brought back bad childhood memories. Clive went with me to the hospital where I was prepared for the operation.

I was awakened from my drug-induced sleep by a gentle tapping on my face. It was Doctor Ferris.

"You have a beautiful baby boy Kim, he weighs 6 lb 14 oz and before you ask, he's a perfectly healthy strong boy!"

After about four hours, I was sitting up in bed looking for my baby son!

"When he is due his next feed can I give it to him?" I asked.

The nurse seemed a little surprised that I wanted to get on with things so soon after my operation, but I really wanted to be involved as soon as possible. I had been told previously, by a doctor, that to lie too long after an operation meant your body started to stiffen, I didn't want that to happen, not when I had so much to do!

In practice though, it was a little tougher than I had imagined. After a Caesarean, you imagine that if you laugh, you will burst open! Manoeuvring myself into my wheelchair was a nightmare! I started by pulling myself towards the end of the bed, with my back facing the wheelchair. I then held both my legs tightly with my right hand to make sure they didn't fall and pull on my stitches, then with my left hand, I would pull myself slowly towards the wheelchair!

The nurses persistently offered their assistance, but I politely refused.

"I won't have your help at home, I need to do this myself, I want to be independent."

They understood, and watched nervously as I heaved myself in and out of the chair. I fed 'Allan' as we agreed to call our baby, as often as I could, the nappies were a challenge to say the least, I simply couldn't master the art of putting the pin in right!

When I went home to Mum's house where we were staying while we sorted out accommodation for ourselves, the problem of how to transport Allan in and out of the car presented itself.

Clive had found work locally and Mum and Dad both worked. My sister Elizabeth had recently moved to Lisburn and I had every intention of making frequent visits to my new niece, not to mention showing off my new baby to Frances and Beatrice too!

I refused to be beaten. I soon got over the problem of transporting Allan from the house to the car. I wrapped him in extra blankets to pad him well, then I put him deep down into his baby nest.

Then with Allan in my arms, I'd bump my rear down the two steps into the drive way. Once on level ground I'd place Allan on the ground and then pull the baby nest gently towards the car with my teeth! I had the whole procedure down to a fine art! But I still couldn't get the darned nappy-pin in right without stabbing myself!

On Friday's, Elizabeth and I headed for the local shopping centre with Allan and Baby Kim in tow. Both babies would lie on my knee, as I held them close with my left hand, while Elizabeth pushed the trolley with me holding on to the trolley with my right hand. People often remarked as to how we coped with the trolley of shopping and two children and a wheelchair!

Another assumption people usually made was that the two children were twins, and were Elizabeths! She didn't take too kindly to this, taking it as an insult to me, so she was forever telling people.

"The little girl is mine and the little boy is hers!"

On one particular shopping trip, a minor miracle happened. Halfway down aisle four (the baby needs aisle, our favourite!) I spotted a huge 'new' display.

"Bring me over there, what does that sign say? DISPOSABLE NAPPIES?? Happy days!!"

From that day on, there wasn't one task I couldn't do as well as anyone, including putting a nappy on!

One morning, on the way to Elizabeth's house, my car broke down. I sat by the roadside with my 'disabled illuminated sign' (a glass disabled logo which plugged into the cigarette lighter and flashed). I was helpless, no one came to my aid for what seemed an eternity! I felt vulnerable for the first time in my life, not for myself, I had a baby to think about now. Fortunately an army land rover pulled over in front of me and helped me to find a garage. I was really grateful, but it made me think about going out alone!

When I am sitting in my car I look as normal as the next person, so people can be forgiven for assuming I can do everything myself. However, I was once stopped by a police officer during a heavy security cordon. The troubles had been particularly intense and the security forces were searching cars at checkpoints.

"Please step out of your car madam and open your boot," the police officer demanded.

"I'm sorry, I can't."

"I'll ask you once more madam, step out of your car."

"I would if I could, but I can't" I said as I reluctantly pulled my skirt above my foot and wiggled my foot. (I hated to have to do that!)

The officer was very apologetic and offered to help me through the traffic jam, but I wouldn't have that, how was he to know? I didn't want special treatment. I wouldn't even use my yellow disabled sticker, somehow it was like admitting I was different, and I didn't feel different, I was just like anyone else as far as I was concerned! I think because I had so many brothers and sisters, I felt I was 'normal' but when I became older, other people, who don't know me, see me as different.

If I wanted to see what a dress was like, I would ask Beatrice to try it on for me. I loved seeing how it would look worn 'standing up' Since Allan was born, I no longer wore my limbs, it was too uncomfortable, besides, I could manage better on ground level! I would pick out a dress I liked, and Beatrice would go into a dressing room and try it on.

"Give us a twirl," I'd say as she came out to let me see 'my' dress.

"O yes, I like that one, but it'll look much better with my figure in it!" I'd laugh.

Once I decided to buy the dress Beatrice pushed me over to the counter to pay. I would hand over the money, and invariably the assistant would talk to Beatrice and offer her the change! This made Beatrice mad, she hated it when shop assistants did that! It really is unbelievable how many people there are who still think that if someone is in a wheelchair, they must be brain dead!

My pet hate is when someone treats me like a two year old puppy and strokes my head while making soothing noises and talking about me as if I can't hear! I find it amusing, but woe betide the one who does it in full view of one of my family! Ditto anyone who parks in a disabled space and jumps out of their car like Linford

Christie! One of my siblings will be after you, so you'd better be Linford Christie!

While Clive and I were looking for somewhere to live, Mum and Dad were arguing more and more. We really wanted to find somewhere of our own. When we finally found a bungalow we liked, it was only yards from the family home.

There was a big snag. To buy our bungalow, the trust insisted the family home had to be sold, to pay for the new house. I hadn't bargained on that, neither had Mum and Dad when they had given up a perfectly good home on advice from the trust, to invest my money in property, now they would have no home!

I felt dreadful, what a predicament to be in! For me to buy a home for Clive, Allan and myself, I would be effectively making my parents homeless! We talked about it. Mum said there was nothing to worry about, they would find somewhere, but I knew Mum and Dad had put a lot of their own money into the house. We agreed to sell and for Mum and Dad to get a small deposit for another house.

By the time the house was sold and I moved into my new bungalow, Mum and Dad had separated! It was a sad time for the whole family, but no real surprise as things had been bad for a long time between them. Mum lived with me for a while and Dad spent time between Frances and Beatrice. Eventually Mum bought a small house, and Dad found a flat.

We soon settled down. I loved having my own home! I enjoyed choosing furniture and seemed to have a flair for interior decorating. I loved to have everything matching, right down to the last detail.

A few months after we moved in I discovered I was pregnant again. We were delighted. Beatrice started coming up every day to help me with the housework, especially the ironing. I found it difficult to iron for any length of time. Clive was working and I was glad of the company since Mum had moved. Frances, Beatrice and I had some good laughs over tea and cream buns! Elizabeth had gone back to England and Joan was there too. We enjoyed our get togethers as our family was reduced considerably for a while, so we made the most of our time together.

On 7th October, 1982, my second son, Russell was born, again by Caesarean section. He was a healthy, normal baby and we were delighted. Allan was two now, and he was looking forward to seeing his new baby brother.

I wasn't so fortunate with my section scar this time though. On the third day, the nurse came around to remove the stitches, it seemed the scar was healing too quickly! On the 6th day, the remaining stitches were removed. After two weeks, my stomach burst open! It was horrible, the wound became badly infected for the next three weeks I had to have the wound packed with gauze .... YUK!

A very close relative of Clive's had come over from England to stay while I had Russell, I was upset at her reaction when she heard I had had another boy, I knew she wanted Clive to have a girl, but I was hurt when she coldly declared, "Huh! another boy!"

I was managing quite well and getting into a good routine, when something happened which changed my whole way of life. The local news had a report about a body being dumped in a car boot outside a local factory. It was the factory where Clive worked! For the next few days, Clive was worried about going into work. He had a distinct English accent, he was worried someone might single him out as an ex-soldier, it was a dangerous situation.

I started to imagine all sorts of things happening, at that time anything was possible, every day someone was being buried due to a terrorist killing! Clive wanted to go home to England, I agreed, my family came first!

We went over to England to look at houses and found one we really liked, we put a deposit down, and put our own house up for sale. Mum was devastated, she didn't want me to go, Beatrice tried to talk me out of it,

"You'll hate it over there, you're a homebird Kim, think about it!" she pleaded.

Frances talked to me and advised me not to go. My mind was made up, if there was the slightest chance that anything was going to happen to Clive, then we had to go! They all understood, and helped me to organise everything, there were tears as we sailed away, but I knew there would be lots of visits.

We settled into our new home. It was a brand new house in a new development in Burnley, Lancashire. I started to make new friends almost as soon as we moved. My phone bills were huge though, I needed to hear familiar voices, I wanted to keep up with all the news from home, I was homesick, but I would never admit it!

Beatrice and Billy came over for a visit the first summer we were there, they brought their new baby Michael. I had been used to Beatrice having only two children and found it odd to see her with a baby again! It was lovely to see them and we had a great week together!

Clive started working for his father in a plumbing firm. I began to try to become a little closer to Clive's family. It wasn't easy. I was an Irish girl with an Irish accent, I stood out a mile, but I was determined not to let a little thing like that stand in my way!

I called around to his mother's home one day to bring the boys to see their Grandmother. She seemed edgy, but was pleasant enough to the boys, so I didn't let it annoy me. However, while I was strapping my seatbelt on to leave she said,

"Call again, but next time leave it until it's dark, I don't want the neighbours to see, you understand don't you?"

I understood only too well. When I arrived home I cried my heart out.

One morning in late December 1984 I went out into my hall to pick up my usual copy of the 'Sun' newspaper. As I read the headline I could hardly finish reading the story I was so overwhelmed with emotion.

There in front of me was a picture of an angelic little baby girl. She had been born without arms and legs and her parents had decided to give her away as they couldn't cope with her condition!

I was dreadfully upset, especially when I read that the baby's mother had said she would have preferred if 'baby Tina' had been born with 'downs syndrome' or better still ... dead! For the first time in my life I phoned a newspaper. With a mixture of emotion and anger, I spoke to the newspaper office about the story I had just read.

"How can this woman even think of giving her baby away? All baby Tina needs is her Mother's love!" I said, my voice warbling with emotion.

I explained that I too had been born without legs and shortened arms, yet my family had loved me. I eventually offered to pass on my mother's phone number so Tina's mum could talk to someone who had been through the same dilemma.

As I calmed down, I realised that the Mother must be going through hell. I felt sure that she would soon accept her baby, I prayed she would!

Later on that same day, a Sun reporter arrived to interview me and take photographs of me with Allan and Russell. They took details of my family life and thanked me for my interest in the story of baby Tina. They explained that they had hundreds of people responding to the story, everyone was saddened by the plight of the beautiful little baby born without arms and legs.

Next morning the front of the page was dominated by little Tina. It seemed half of Britain wanted to adopt her! She had captured the hearts of everyone. Hundreds had phoned offering Tina a home with them. Others promised cash, or gifts to help her parents cope. Other disabled people besides myself had phoned with messages for the parents not to despair!

On pages four and five a double page spread reported on the numerous people who had phoned to offer support and encouragement. A large picture of myself with Allan and Russell stared back at me! The report read as follows:

ALL TINA NEEDS IS LOVE
Kim's message of hope for Mother Jeanette

Courageous Kim Whitford, who was born without legs, pleaded with little Tina Morris' mum yesterday;
"Don't give her up. Giver her a chance ... give her your love."
Thalidomide victim, Kim, wept when she read that Jeanette Morris planned to have tragic Tina fostered.
Jeanette, 25, could not bear the prospect of raising a child with no arms or legs.
But 22 year old Kim, a proud mother of two young boys said yesterday:

"I was one of the lucky ones because my family wanted me despite my deformities. I'll never forget the moment my mother told me simply, 'We loved you from the moment you were born.' Baby Tina must have a mother's love. It's no use saying other people can give her better care and attention. That is impossible."

Kim weighed 6lb 5oz when she was born in Belfast on June 25, 1962. The horrifying effect of Thalidomide also left her with deformed hands. At seven months she was given her first 'legs', ski-like shoes on which she would shuffle around.

She became a professional country and western singer and toured the states and Canada. At 17, she met her husband Clive at a Belfast disco. He was serving as a soldier in the trouble-torn city. The devoted young couple now live in a four-bedroomed bungalow in Worsthorne, Burnley, Lancs. with their boys Russell two and four year old Allan. Kim said:

"My disability never came between me and Clive. We knew we were the perfect match from the start. And we both adore our two sons. My mum never thought there was a chance I would get married, but it happened and it could happen to baby Tina later in life. With artificial limbs she could get around and live an almost normal life."

Kim's own lust for life is based on this principle:

"People may look at me because I am deformed, but it doesn't bother me, I don't care what people think!"

Kim drives an automatic Ford Escort, but when she can't motor somewhere she thinks nothing of being carried on her husband's back. She also loves playing badmington with 26 year old Clive who is now a lorry driver. Kim added;

"The only thing I regret is not being able to run around the park with the kids, I have got artificial legs ... I am 5 ft 4 ins with them and 3ft nothing without them! But they help give me independence. Everybody in the world should be given a chance ... and that chance means the love of parents."

The report also had a message from another thalidomide victim called Tina, telling the mother not to give up hope. Tina was also born (as a victim of Thalidomide) without arms or legs. She said her mother had not given up hope, for her mother's words of encouragement were;

"It's been a struggle, but it's been worth it!"

Another couple had adopted a baby with almost identical disabilities, they said their little boy was a source of joy and happiness in their lives.

For a few days little Tina was headline news, but their mother give her up for fostering. The last I heard, she was still being fostered and her mother was expecting another baby.

I was very saddened to hear that the baby Tina had lost her mother, but I realised how lucky I had been to have been born into such a loving family. I phoned my Mother to talk to her, I suddenly felt the need to hear her voice.

Soon, everything was back to routine and we settled back into normal family life.

We celebrated Christmas at home with my family. We had a wonderful holiday and I was happy to see everyone. We brought in the new year with a party at Mum's house, it was 1985! I had mixed emotions when it came time to go back to England.

Later near the end of the Summer, I discovered I was expecting another baby. Clive and I were delighted! We had two lovely boys and another baby would complete our family. My pregnancy was fairly normal, I would have to have another Caesarean, and my doctor had told me that three Caesareans was as many as I could have. It wasn't recommended for anyone to have more than that!

One day as I stood in the kitchen, the door opened and there stood my sister Beatrice! I almost fainted with the shock!

"Where did you come from? How did you get here?!"

"I thought I would surprise you and by the look on your face, I have!" she laughed.

Beatrice told me she had phoned Clive to arrange for him to pick her up at the Liverpool ferry, so she could visit me and see how I was coping. I was really pleased to see a familiar face and hear an Irish accent! Unfortunately she could only stay overnight as she had to be back home the next day, but I caught up on a lot of news from back home.

As arranged, I went into hospital to have my baby. The last few weeks had been difficult as with most pregnancies, but I was anxious as my Mother-in-law had told Clive not to even bother phoning to tell her about the baby unless it was a girl! I could hardly believe it! I was very upset, we'd already picked a boy's name and a girl's name, it didn't matter to us what we had, I couldn't understand why it was so important to her!

When I awoke from the anaesthetic, Clive told me we had another beautiful son! As usual, my first question was;

"Is everything okay?"

Clive looked very grim, I could tell there was something wrong! As the tears rolled down his cheeks, he cried as he spoke,

"Marc (the name we had picked for our son) has an extra thumb!"

"What else is wrong with him?" I demanded to know!

"Nothing as far as they can tell."

"Are you absolutely sure?"

"Yes, I promise," Clive replied.

"Promise?"

"Promise!"

"Well, if that's all there is wrong with him, it can be easily rectified" I said calmly.

Clive looked at me with a puzzled expression, he couldn't believe I was taking it so calmly, I closed my eyes and drifted off to sleep.

I learned later that Clive had phoned my Mum to tell her that she had a new grandson, but was unable to speak on the phone as he had broken down in tears as soon as she had answered the phone. He found it impossible to tell her about the extra thumb. Of course, Mum was worried as to how I would cope with it, she needn't have worried, I was taking it in my stride, but Clive seemed devastated.

Meanwhile, my brother Trevor had bought a present for baby Marc along with a 'new baby' card. It had a picture of a little baby boy on it and read:

"10 little fingers, 10 little toes, congratulations on the birth of your baby boy!"

Mum said that on hearing about Marc's extra thumb, Trevor had torn the card to shreds and cried.

"Why did it have to happen to our Kim's child? Out of the seven of us, why did it happen to our Kim?"

I was amazed at everyone's reaction, after all, it could have been so much worse.

"So what! My son was beautiful no matter what! Surely it was better he was born with something extra instead of having something missing?"

I knew it would only be a matter of Marc having an operation to have the little thumb amputated. One thing the doctors thought strange though, there was a fully formed bone in the thumb, but they assured us the operation when Marc was older would be routine. With all the fuss Clive 'forgot' to phone his parents to tell them the news. I think he was as upset as I was about his mother's cruel re-mark, after all, she didn't want to know, it was only another boy after all!

Allan and Russell loved having another brother, and we soon forgot about the drama surrounding his birth. He was perfect in every other way. We were thankful for that, and our family was complete.

Marc was a loving, gentle child who was always eager to please. He loved to draw and 'write' me little stories while Allan and Russell attended school. The doctors decided to amputate the thumb before Marc started school.

When Marc was two-and-a-half years old the hospital sent an appointment for him to have the operation. We started to talk to him to prepare him for the hospital. When the day came, we had a phone call from the hospital just as we were about to leave for the journey there.

"We're very sorry to inform you, but there is no bed for Marc, the operation will have to be postponed."

I was livid, here we were all ready to go, Marc had had nothing to eat as we had been instructed not to allow him anything before the anaesthetic!

A couple of weeks later, another date was set. This time there was no hitch, the operation went ahead as planned. When Marc awoke, he was crying so much it broke my heart.

As I rushed over to comfort him, the nurse said.

"Don't worry, I'll give him a little injection for the pain."

"You will not! He's only crying with hunger, he hasn't had anything to eat for 15 hours!" I snapped.

The nurse left and appeared five minutes later with some toast and jam for Marc. He sat on my knee and ate the lot and never cried again. It must have been painful for him and he was so tiny, but I was very proud of his courage. His hand had to be tied to the bed to help the swelling go down, he never complained once, he had the patience of a saint! When he was allowed out of the bed to play, he had to hold his hand high in the air, he looked so comical!

During my times in hospital, I had seen many children suffer after operations, I admired so many of them for their courage and spirit, they could put many adults to shame! Marc made a full recovery and was left with only a very small scar where the thumb had been.

In November of 1988, I received a phone call from an American woman called Lois Lipman. She was a journalist for CBS news in America, working on the '60 minutes' documentary programme.

She explained that the film crew were in England making a programme entitled 'Thalidomide 25 years on'. She asked if I would be prepared to talk to an interviewer about my life and family. I was surprised and delighted to take part in the programme. We arranged to meet and talk provisionally, so we could both clarify what was expected from each other.

I drove to the railway station to pick Lois up. We talked during the journey and got on well together. The programme makers were interested in doing a full interview including filming my daily life with my family. I had never talked so much about myself, but I thoroughly enjoyed the experience!

The crew were a friendly group, and made me feel relaxed. When the filming was completed, they promised me a video tape of the finished programme, as the actual documentary would only be transmitted in America, Israel and Germany.

When the local paper heard about the filming going on at my home, they sent a reporter out to my home to interview me! A short report appeared that week in the local paper so all in all I had a very eventful week!

Soon it was Christmas again and we had a great time with the children as they were at such a wonderful age. Allan was seven, Russell was five and Marc was almost three. Santa was good to each of them and we had happy joyful children chattering from the wee small hours! All our preparations were well worth it just to see their little faces, everything seemed perfect. I was really happy although I still missed my family especially at Christmas. I had made quite a few friends in the five years I had lived in Burnley.

As 1989 arrived, I had high hopes for the new year as everyone does. My home was newly decorated and every room was furnished exactly the way I had pictured them way back when we first moved in. This was the year when I decided I would try to find something to occupy my days, I thought perhaps some voluntary work, as Marc was starting nursery school, I wanted to do something useful.

My hopes and dreams were short-lived, fate had other plans for me, 1989 was not going to be a good year for me.

CHAPTER THIRTEEN

Unlucky for some!

I remember so well the night my marriage crumbled. We had just been out for the evening with friends. The show was a compilation of songs from Andrew Lloyd-Webber musicals. During the show, my husband and my friend appeared to be going to the toilet at the same time. I knew then that all my fears were justified. For a while I had suspected something was going on, but I put it to the back of my mind, now I had to confront the reality, I couldn't deny it any longer.

On the way home, I said to my husband,

"You're having an affair, aren't you?"

He flatly denied it. As we turned into our street, I noticed a strange car with a Northern Ireland registration plate parked in our driveway. Mum had arrived on a surprise visit. She had been in Sheffield attending my Uncle's funeral and had driven up to surprise me. We pretended everything was fine, we didn't have to pretend for long as Mum was very tired from the journey and retired to bed after about half an hour.

Once again I asked if Clive was having an affair, he denied it again. He asked me why I thought he was having an affair. I couldn't explain why, it was just a feeling deep inside, a feeling of doom.

"What would you do if I was having an affair?" he asked.

"It would have to be the end of our marriage," I said, the pit of my stomach weighing heavily.

"I'm not having an affair! I'm not having an AFFAIR! but I am in love with Mary," he declared.

He then walked out, taking nothing but our pet dog. Needless to say, I was in pieces. I was thrown into a complete turmoil. I went upstairs to wake my Mum, grateful that she was there for me to turn to. I told her what had happened, and we sat up all night. I cried for a full 24 hours and heard nothing from Clive.

When I eventually heard from him, I wanted him to come home so badly it hurt. I just couldn't believe everything was over. Had it not been for my Mum, I don't know what I would have done. She helped me to put things into perspective. Things would never be the same, Clive had made his decision. I had to sort myself out before our feelings for each other turned to hate.

Within ten days my whole life changed. I lost my home, my friends, my life in England, although leaving England wasn't too hard to bear. The six years I had spent there seemed to have been boring, lonely and confusing for me. I missed the warmth, and company of my family and being part of a normal family circle.

My husband's family had made no secret of the fact that they did not like me. Once when I called around to visit, I was asked not to call in future, unless it was dark, in case the neighbours saw me. People like that I could live without!

Mum helped me as much as she could. She took me to a solicitor to make sure I would be looked after concerning my home and children. As Mum arrived at the airport, my sister Beatrice was arriving to stay with me. When Beatrice left, Frances, my oldest sister arrived. They made sure I was not alone for even one minute. They helped me to pack up my belongings and organise everything.

I left England with Frances and my three children. They were surprisingly well behaved. I don't think they fully realised what was happening, may be it was better they didn't know yet, it would be hard enough telling them. For the time being they were so excited at the prospect of living near their Granny and Aunts and Uncles and cousins, nothing else seemed to matter to them.

When I finally arrived in Northern Ireland I broke down. It was somehow final and complete. It took me a long time to settle down. I went to live with my sister Beatrice and her family. Although it wasn't home, I knew I was welcome there and I knew if I needed to talk to someone or a shoulder to cry on, they would be there for me.

The first couple of months were a blur to me. The children were being emotionally neglected because I couldn't focus. I didn't have any time for them. Beatrice was looking after their meals and putting them to bed and all the things children needed, but what they really needed at the time was their Mum. After all they had already lost their father. I never gave them kisses and hugs, I could only think of what I was going through. I was consumed with what had happened to my marriage. I couldn't sleep or eat. I was a mess. My weight went down to two-and-a-half stone, I was on the verge of giving up.

One morning I woke and thought,

"Kim, get a hold on your life, you've fought worse than this, now you are going to give it all up over one person who isn't worth it."

I physically brushed myself down, rubbed my hands together and said out loud,

"Right, let's get on with it!"

From that moment, I became the person I once was, cheerful, and glad to be alive. The children got their mother back, my family had their sister back. I went out twice a week, I looked up old friends and generally enjoyed life to the full. I realised how many people care for me and what a mistake it had been to leave my family to live in England in the first place. I went from a loving secure caring close family, to 'a black hole' in England. I realised how miserable I had been for six years and how glad I was to be home. I didn't want to leave there the way I had, but at last I was home where I was loved.

When I felt stronger, I realised how foolish I had been to leave my home and contents with Clive, especially as I was hearing reports about Mary visiting my home. My brother Trevor encouraged me to hire a van and go to England to retrieve my furniture. We set off on the ferry and arrived around lunchtime. We worked at removing what we could. Angela, Trevor's wife answered the door to find a casserole on the doorstep (obviously meant for Clive). She promptly walked over to Mary's house and tipped it over her doorstep! It was obvious from the state of the house that they were very much at home among my possessions.

What I couldn't fit into the van, I gave away to the neighbours, a three piece suite, various items were given freely,. However, the more I searched through the house, the angrier I got! I emptied all of Clive's clothes into a black bin bag, I was taking everything! As Clive put his key into the door, he was visibly shocked when he saw us. But not as shocked as he was going to be. I told him that I had left his belongings in the garage. As we drove off, I felt stronger and better than I had for a long time.

A picture of Clive walking into the garage to collect his 'belongings' came into my mind. Earlier on, I had found some old records of mine. I love country and western, especially Patsy Cline and Connie Frances. I had quite a collection. One of Connie's songs seemed perfect for the occasion.

An old gramophone-style record player was in the garage, I placed one record on the turn table and left the 'arm' over so the record would play repeatedly over and over again. A smile came across my face as I visualised Clive opening the garage door to hear Connie belting out,

"WHO'S SORRY NOW? .... WHO'S SORRY NOW?"

I know it's terrible to admit it, but it felt good, and I hadn't felt good in a long time! I knew now why Clive had become so fashion conscious all of a sudden and I had paid for a whole new Summer wardrobe for him so he could look good for another woman.

I had spent my 26th birthday in a haze, when I arrived back at Beatrice's house, I would have to cope with the children on my own for the first time, there was no way around it.

I was in the process of looking at properties, but until I found somewhere to live, I was going to stay at Beatrice's house while she moved into her new home 40 miles away. Mum, Frances and Trevor lived 20 miles away. I was completely alone. It was scary, but the children became very close to me, I suppose in a way they had missed me while I was away in another world of darkness and despair. I knew I had to be strong for their sake if not my own.

It wasn't too long before I found a new home. Mum was moving to a new house and I decided to buy her house. Mum had remarried and was starting afresh. Her house was perfect for us and we were settled by mid-October.

Christmas was very different from last year, but I promised myself 1990 would be a happy year for me and my children. I cried a lot, but I had made my decision. Clive had visited just before I moved into Mum's house. He wanted to talk to me so I agreed to meet him. He said he had made a terrible mistake and wanted to get together again. He wanted to live in Belfast with me and the children. I told him I couldn't go back to him, I had made my decision, so I spent Christmas without my husband and the children had no father to show them how to work their toys, but I just knew things would be better somehow.

CHAPTER FOURTEEN

One parent family

As time passed, and the children started to become involved with school activities, things seemed to be almost normal. I began to go out with some old school friends. The house where I lived was close to where I had attended school in my teens and everywhere I went, I seemed to bump into an old school pal!

It felt good to see so many friends and we arranged to go out. I arranged a baby-sitter and left to go to a dance. My confidence was low, I was now in a wheelchair all the time, as I hadn't worn my limbs since the boys had been born. I wondered if anyone would take the time to get to know me instead of seeing the wheelchair and dismissing me out of hand as just 'someone in a wheelchair'. How would anyone find me attractive. Time would tell I told myself.

As it happened, men seemed to accept me for myself, instead of my method of transport. My confidence, which had taken a nose dive was beginning to surface again. One night I had three offers of a date! Some of the men I turned down looked at me strangely as if they were doing me a favour asking me, and I had the audacity to say no!

They couldn't understand someone in a wheelchair turning them down, and giving them the cold shoulder, but why shouldn't I be able to choose who I wanted to go out with the same as anyone else?

One night, I was sitting in a club, near to where I had lived as a very young child. A man came over and introduced himself to me.

"Hello Kim, I remember you from way back, I used to love to see you coming to the local shops."

"What do you mean you loved to see me coming?"

"Well, I always admired your independence and courage, as you walked to the shops by yourself."

"I remember an occasion when you were about five years old, do you?" he enquired with a grin on his face.

"No, I don't think I do."

"Well I rushed over to you to pick you up after you had fallen, but you told me in no uncertain terms to 'take off'", you would get up by yourself."

My face reddened as I laughed in embarrassment, I couldn't remember the incident at all!

He sat down beside me and we talked well into the night, much to the disgust of my boyfriend who had been sitting beside me the whole evening! The guy's name was Eddie, I found I had a lot in common with him and I really liked him.

We became firm friends over the next few months. Eddie started to call at my house almost on a weekly basis. He said he just dropped in on his way to the ice rink and it also turned out that his Uncle lived in the next street to mine!

We often sat for ages just talking about characters we knew when we lived in Taughmonagh, the estate where we had both grown up. I enjoyed reminiscing about those days and Eddie had a good memory for detail. We laughed about the incident where he had tried to rescue me, it seemed I had found a good friend and I looked forward to his visits.

At the time, Eddie was involved with a woman, but he confided to me that the relationship was very turbulent. His girlfriend had become verbally abusive and had started throwing his clothes outside in the garden on a regular basis! I was still seeing my boy-friend, but I was becoming unhappy for other reasons. My boyfriend was much younger than I was and we seemed to have nothing in common, he was a decent guy, but things were just not right so we finished.

My friendship with Eddie grew stronger as time passed and when he told me he had ended his relationship, I was pleased as I knew he was unhappy, but the last thing on my mind was getting involved again!

One evening I took two thalidomide friends of mine to the club where I had met Eddie. I had known both men since I was three years old. Near the end of the night, a disagreement started between both of them. I was to be the driver that night, and they were arguing over who would be dropped off last!

The argument moved on as they argued over who had fancied me first! I became deeply embarrassed as I didn't want to offend either of them, they were long term friends, but I was in a dilemma, the whole situation was getting ridiculous!When they both left to use the toilet, I told Eddie about the row which had been brewing. I asked if he would follow me to my house first, then drive with me to drop my two friends off. I hoped that by doing it that way I would save any embarrassing situation arising! He readily agreed to help ... my hero!

From that night on, we became a couple, everything seemed to be right for us, he finally confessed that he hadn't been ice skating for months and he hadn't visited his Uncle in years! Within 7 months we were engaged to be married!

I wanted our wedding to be perfect. I phoned numerous churches to ask if they would marry a divorced couple. Most of them refused, we visited many of the churches to ask personally but it seemed futile. I desperately wanted to be married in a church. Eventually I found a small church just off the Newtownards Road in Belfast where the minister said he would be happy to marry us, I was ecstatic!

Beatrice and Mum went with me to help choose my wedding dress. I chose a bridal pink satin gown with a frilled train, I wanted to walk down the aisle, I was determined.

The wedding was to take place on 3rd July, 1995, there was no time to lose, I had to get back into those limbs. I told Eddie there was no way I would go down the aisle in my wheelchair! I had to walk.

It had been thirteen years since I had last worn my artificial limbs. I contacted the limb-fitting centre at Musgrave Hospital and asked if they could make me a new pair of limbs. They started work on my new limbs immediately. As the limbs neared completion, I still hadn't mastered the balance! I felt sure it was the new limbs, and not me! I had perfect balance all those years ago, I had to get it back again.

The doctor told me I would simply have to resign myself to the fact that I would never walk on limbs again.

"After such a long period of time without limbs, you could never learn to balance the way you used to, I'm sorry Kim," he said.

That was it! Like a red flag to a bull, he had said the magic words! I would just have to prove him wrong!

Eddie found an old pair of my limbs in the attic, he cleaned them up and dusted them down. I'd show them! Two days later I was at Musgrave Park Hospital. I sat down between a set of parallel bars which were used to help steady artificial limb users while they learned to balance. I began to lace the legs up and as I finished preparing the limbs, I closed my eyes and prayed;

"Please God, let me find my balance, let me walk down that aisle."

As I lifted myself off the chair onto my feet, I steadied myself before I started. The first couple of steps were a little uneasy, in no time though, it was as if I'd never been without them! I walked through the parallel bars and over to the doctor and limb technician. I stood in front of them and said cheekily;

"Told you, you were wrong!"

"Are you sure it's been 13 years since you last walked, Kim?" the doctor asked.

"Positive!"

"Well, your balance is perfect, I can't believe it, I really can't!" he admitted.

I opened the door of the fitting room and proceeded to walk down the corridor by myself. My confidence was growing by the second. As I neared the reception area, Annie, Jim and the others who had been in the centre for many years and had known me as a young child, clapped with delight and said,

"It's nice to see the old Kim back! You always like to prove you could do anything you put your mind to!"

I practised as often as I could, the limbs no longer fitted me properly, but if I could bear them on just long enough to get to the reception, I would be happy with that!

When I arrived home, we began to plan exactly what we both wanted on our wedding day. Allan, Russell and Marc were sitting watching television, but were hanging on our every word. Allan got up and came over to sit beside me. I knew he had something on his mind.

"Mum I would like to give you away at your wedding, can I go please, I really want to be there?"

I really wanted the boys to be at the wedding, but I explained to Allan that he was a little too young to give me away, but he could be ring-bearer. He was thrilled to bits. I asked Russell what he would like to do. Being the wittiest of my trio of boys, he put his innocent Macauley Culkin expression on and said cheekily;

"You want us three kids running around you on your wedding day? .... I don't think so!"

It was a headache to arrange for everyone to go to the bridal salon. My niece Kim, who was living in England, was coming over on her own for a holiday, so I decided to try and set a date while she was here when everyone could meet to go for a fitting.

Mum, Beatrice and my nieces Kim and Lynsey agreed on a date and time. Unfortunately, my young niece Lauren, who was to do flower girl was in Germany so it was impossible to arrange for her to be with us. Joan sent her measurements though, it was the best she could do.

The evening before we were all due to meet, the phone rang;

"Kim, I don't think I'll be able to make it tomorrow," Beatrice said.

"You'd better make it, young Kim is going home the day after tomorrow, it can't be another day!"

"I know, I know, I've arranged for Lynsey to have a day off school and everything but something has happened."

"What is so important? .... you have to! Come on Beatrice, I've done a lot of organising for this."

"I'm on crutches!"

"Yeah, right, pull the other one, you really had me going there for a minute!"

"I'm not kidding, Kim. I think I've torn a calf muscle, I'm really on crutches, I couldn't walk into town, I can hardly get down the hall!"

"No problem! You can sit on my wheelchair, there's room for both of us if we sit tight!"

"You're kidding aren't you?"

"I'm perfectly serious, you're coming and that's the end of the story."

Beatrice knew I wasn't joking so she reluctantly agreed to go ahead as planned.

We all met up, and sure enough Beatrice arrived with a pair of crutches, with Lynsey holding both handbags. When we reached the bridal salon, another obstacle presented itself. The fitting room for brides was on the top floor, and before me was the steepest set of stairs I'd ever seen.

Usually Beatrice would carry me on her back, but that was out of the question! Luckily Lynsey at 15 was a strong girl and she kneeled down and carried me piggyback style up to the top floor. We were a real sight for sore eyes, as Mum stepped up one at a time precariously, Lynsey was directly behind Mum with me on her back and last, and definitely the most pathetic of the motley crew, was Beatrice hopping up each step with a very inelegant 'kerplunk!' worthy of Long John Silver!

I thought the uppity assistant was going to swoon when she caught sight of us at the entrance of the bridal room! Once we were organised, the assistant brought me a selection of gowns to try on. Lynsey tried them on for me (a favourite trick of mine to help me see what the dress would look like before I tried it on).

I had provisionally left over a pink bridal dress on a previous visit, and I just wanted to see a couple of others just to be sure. Once we had chosen the bridesmaids' dresses to match my pink dress, my mind was made up.

By the time we left, we were all tired and hungry. Beatrice's leg was getting worse, she could barely put her foot to the ground so she agreed to sit on my wheelchair, while Lynsey pushed the both of us towards McDonalds. The two of us laughed and giggled the whole way up Royal Avenue, as people turned to look at us. We must have looked ridiculous! I was sitting back in my wheelchair, while Beatrice sat sideways holding onto her crutches cringing with embarrassment, but unable to stop laughing. Anyone looking at us must have thought there was one person in the wheelchair with two heads, as my head was the only part of me visible!

When we finally arrived at McDonalds, we were a wretched heap, we all needed to use the loo! As we manoeuvred into the cubicle, me first, then Beatrice balancing on her crutches, we laughed again until we almost cried. When we emerged from the exterior door of the ladies, there was a queue of people with bemused looks on their faces, they must have heard everything we had said! We ate our meals discreetly and left by the nearest available exit!

Soon, the replies started to arrive. My eldest brother, Alex, sent his apologises, he was still out in Hong Kong, and couldn't make it to my wedding. Everyone else could make it, so I started making the final arrangements.

Russell and Marc wanted to go on holiday with their Dad so I reluctantly let them go. It had been arranged some time ago and the boys were looking forward to going to the Isle of Wight.

As the day drew nearer, I began to feel nervous about walking on my limbs. None of Eddie's family had ever seen me any other way than in my wheelchair. I had almost convinced myself I would fall over and make a fool of myself!

I arose very early on the morning of my wedding. Elizabeth and her husband, Dave, were staying with me, and the household was buzzing! The phone rang, it was Russell and Marc calling from England.

"Have a nice day Mum and good luck!" said Russell.

"Good luck Mummy and Eddie too!" Marc added.

While I was at the hairdressers, Allan pulled the little saying off the calendar for 3rd July, 1992. He gave it to Eddie.

"This is for you Eddie."

Eddie read the verse. "Anyone can be a father, but not everyone can be a Dad." He was deeply touched by the token of affection and he had tears in his eyes when he told me about it. I was very proud of Allan.

Elizabeth, Kim and Allan accompanied me over to Mum's where I was overwhelmed when a beautiful single red rose was delivered for me from Eddie with a simple note attached. It read;

"See you in church. Love Eddie."

On the morning of the wedding everyone arrived at Mum's house to get ready. We were all rushing around trying to make ourselves beautiful when the fresh flowers arrived. We finished our fussing about and headed down the hall for the final approval by Mum. As I left the bedroom, I fell over! Boy did it hurt! My main concern was my dress, luckily it wasn't torn, but I had a nasty fall.

The white Rolls Royce arrived and we set off for the Branagh Memorial Church. Mum's glasses were all steamed up, she had to keep wiping them clear! We arrived at the church and I held on to Mum and my Uncle Jim as I walked up the steps to the church. I steadied myslef as Mum released her hold and walked up the aisle towards Eddie.

As I stood beside Eddie, I looked beside me to see Beatrice with tears streaming down her cheeks, I was okay until I saw her, then I started! We both composed ourselves in time for the minister's opening words though! As we gave and received our vows, Eddie reached over to place the ring on my finger. It refused to go on! I wasn't having that, so I took the ring and pushed it on to my finger myself!

As the pain become worse during the service, I blocked it out. I was determined to enjoy my big day no matter what! The whole day was being captured on video. I had visions of my contorted face being on tape for years to come!

Eddie and I danced to 'unchained melody' for the first dance. As we danced slowly together I whispered to Eddie, "These limbs have got to go, they're killing me!" He swept me up into his arms, and it was such a relief to take the weight off my feet! When he put me back down to earth, the steel bar clicked on my limb bringing back memories of days gone by when my limbs used to break regularly!

Once the reception was well underway, Eddie carried me on his back into our hotel room so I could take the limbs off. I was black and blue!

Sylvia Pavis, the woman who had helped me into singing, sang at our reception while Eddie, not to be outdone sang, 'King of the road' and just to get rid of the last few stragglers, I sang, 'Paper roses'.

We had invited all our friends and family and everyone turned up to share our special day. I was really pleased to have Reverend Harvey there to share my day, as he was a very special friend, and it meant a lot to me. He gave a beautiful speech about my family and our childhood days, and how honoured he was to be present at my wedding. It was my honour to have him there with me!

This time around I knew exactly what I was doing and I was in control of my own life. It really was the best day of my life. We had a wonderful reception and honeymooned in Portugal. I was happier than I had ever been, life was good again!

Eddie's family couldn't have been more welcoming to me. I felt complete and loved, truly loved. I couldn't possibly know what lay in store for me next but whatever lay ahead I was sure I had the strength and support I needed to do battle with bigger and stronger opponents who would know they had been in a fight.

Eddie and I had a wonderful honeymoon and when we returned home to Belfast we still had three weeks alone together as Russell and Marc were staying with their father. Allan had gone on holiday with Elizabeth, Dave and my niece Kim. After his holiday he was going to stay for another two weeks. Kim and Allan were the same age and had become close friends when they were very small.

The time together was bliss although I missed the boys. The house was quiet, very quiet. Whilst looking forward to having the family all back together again. I couldn't help wondering how everything would be now Eddie and I were married.

When we had announced our engagement to the boys, we had talked to them about getting married and what it would mean to all our lives. I spoke to Russell first as he was the one closest to his father.

"How would you feel if Eddie lived here forever, that's what will happen when we get married, we would all share our home, the way Daddy and I used to?"

"I don't mind at all, I like Eddie, and anyway I'd rather have you and Eddie than you and Daddy."

"Why do you say that?"

"Because you and Daddy never seemed to like each other!" he said matter of factly.

Allan shrugged his shoulders;

"It's okay by me Mummy as long as you're happy."

Marc was quite happy with the situation as well, but then he is always easy pleased and pleasant whatever the situation. Time would tell. I had seen and heard children coping with a second marriage, and I knew there would be problems, but I was sure we could cope with whatever came our way. We were best friends as well as husband and wife, and we had talked things over beforehand.

When they arrived home, there were hugs and kisses all round, I was quietly delighted that the boys appeared to have missed Eddie as much as me! The next week was spent buying school uniforms and getting organised for the start of Autumn term. Allan was to start secondary school and I was a little apprehensive. The school he would be attending was the same school that I'd gone to, I hoped he wasn't going to have as dramatic an introduction as I had!

Russell and Marc attended the local primary and they were doing well so I hoped their work would continue to improve. I had heard that the first sign that children are upset can be their school work, indeed I had seen it first-hand when we moved to Belfast. Allan and Russell had to attend a lower grade class, mainly due to the different educational standards between England and Northern Ireland, but there was no denying it, they were not happy little boys for a while.

As it turned out all three boys seemed to be doing well. Allan had the usual difficulties any child has when they make the transition from the safety of primary school to the 'big, bad' secondary system, but all things considered, the birds were singing in the trees and God was in His heaven!

For the first time in a long while I felt secure and not just emotionally so. Since my separation I had been living on an extremely low income. The maintenance payments from Clive were few and far between.

I was actually living on my family allowance since I had moved back to Northern Ireland. While I was still living in Beatrice's house, I had applied for income support. I had been awarded £12 per week, two weeks later the award was withdrawn because I was not entitled to any payment because of my 'trust fund allowance'.

As Beatrice mentioned earlier the trust fund only paid for items I required and I had to write a request to the trust co-ordinator. Anything I received from the trust was paid by cheque, usually to a third party. The social security assumed I had a monthly income from the trust and wouldn't consider giving any allowance to me or the children.

I struggled on borrowing money from Mum on a regular basis. I could have furniture or a new car from the trust, providing I could prove I needed them, but I needed to feed and clothe my children, and there was never any provision for me to do that.

When I had moved into my new house in Belfast I had phoned to ask for a visit from a social security officer. I was sure I must be entitled to something! I had received no money from Clive for 17 weeks and I was desperate. An adjudication officer arrived to see me.

At the time my sister Frances was helping me out in the house. I was entitled to a 'care allowance' paid directly to the carer. With all the filling out of forms due to my new address and other circumstances I had been without my benefit books on and off for a while. I really needed money for essentials!

One of the first questions the officer asked me was about my income.

"At the moment, the only income apart from my trust is ..."

I could barely finish the sentence when he looked straight at me and laughed. It was a patronising, cruel laugh, I was feeling vulnerable, this was vitally important to me, now here was my lifeline being yanked away by this uncaring man sitting in my own front room!

"You have a trust? A trust? There is no way you would be entitled to any money if you have a trust fund!" he laughed.

"But I have no actual money, can I appeal this?"

"No way! You have an income from a trust fund, you have no entitlement to any money from social security."

With this final slap in the face he picked up his briefcase and let himself out. I lay down on the settee and cried, what was I to do? Where would I get money for groceries? It was October 1989, a very low point in my life.

I felt alone, even though I was near my own family, I felt isolated, it was a strange felling, having people around yet feeling alone ... My family tried their best to make sure I was alright but I wanted to do things for myself, I wanted to have my own money and not have to borrow all the time!

From then on I watched every penny, I only bought what I could really afford, which wasn't much, but I managed because I had to.

Chapter Fifteen

Fire hazard? Who me?

When the boys first went to England to visit their father, I told Clive how concerned I was about them seeing him with his girlfriend. They were still fragile after all the upheaval, and I was worried about what they would think of their Dad living with the woman who had once been my friend. He said he understood and would make sure they were not in her company.

Before the house was sold, Clive asked me if I would give him some of the proceeds, £15,000 he suggested. I said I would think about it. However, when the boys came back from their visit and Marc in his innocence talked about sitting on Clive's girlfriend's knee on the train, I seen red!

When he phoned to ask me if the children had arrived safely and hinted about the money he was 'owed' I told him I would keep my 'promise' as he had kept his! Whatever money I had left over after paying for our new home was needed to decorate and furnish, after all, I had left most of my larger furniture items in England! I didn't plan to live hand to mouth any more, my priority now was my children

Now here I was, just three years on, re-married and feeling on top of the world with a man I truly loved and who loved me, what a turnaround! I just knew life would never be the same again ... thank goodness!

For the next few months, we simply got on with our family life, the boys adapted really well, and I was happy visiting my Mum and sisters during the day, and collecting the boys from school. All in all, we were just a normal happy family.

I decided to start going to a further education college, I had always wanted to learn a language, so I decided to begin with German! Full of enthusiasm, I planned to learn French and Spanish later, but German would do to start with! As the weeks went by, more and more people dropped out, the rest of us were disappointed when the tutor explained the class would have to fold due to the lack of numbers.

"I am more than happy to tutor you, but the college has decided the numbers cannot justify paying a tutor, I am sorry," the Swedish tutor explained.

"What about holding the class in my house?" I offered.

"Great idea!"

"I'm game if everyone else is!" seconded another student.

Everyone was enthusiastic, and the tutor agreed to continue the classes in my home. Every Tuesday we met religiously for about three months. Initially we learned German, but the tutor was more and more lax, sometimes arriving a little the worse for drink! He was a nice guy, but as his appearance or lack of it was becoming a hit or miss affair, the group became more social than studious! As often happens, the numbers gradually reduced, and our Tuesday meeting became simply a friendly gathering, and eventually we drifted apart altogether!

One Sunday afternoon, sitting at home bored and restless, I noticed as I read the local paper that the Bruce Lee life story was showing at the MGM picture house in Belfast. I had always been a fan of the early days when Bruce Lee packed the cinema out to the door! I had fond memories of 13 and 14 year-old boys emerging from the latest Bruce Lee film punching and karate kicking the air while letting a high pitched, 'Eee—ee Hai—Yah!'

"Who fancies going to the pictures?" I asked.

"Yes, yes, brilliant!" the boys shouted, obviously as bored as I was.

When everyone was ready, Eddie carried me out to the car as the boys jumped into the back seat, I was really looking forward to the film, I hadn't been to the cinema in ages! The boys were all chatter in the back, and we were all in fine form as we drove the five miles into the centre of town.

"Mum, can we see a different film, we don't fancy the Bruce Lee one?" Russell asked.

"If you promise to behave yourselves, and come straight out when the film is over to wait for Eddie and me if you're out first, you can see another one, deal?"

The boys looked at each other, shrugged their shoulders and said in unison,

"DEAL!"

We parked the car and Allan, as usual, lifted my wheelchair out of the boot and brought it around for me to climb into. As we entered the foyer of the huge cinema, the boys read the posters advertising what was showing in each cinema, they decided to watch 'Homeward Bound'.

"Two adults for Bruce Lee and three children for Homeward Bound please" Eddie said to the cashier.

"Is she going to see Homeward Bound or the Bruce Lee film?"

"The Bruce Lee film," I answered.

The cashier looked straight over my head and spoke to Eddie.

"She can't go into Bruce Lee, it's showing upstairs."

"That's okay, you have a lift haven't you?" answered Eddie.

"Yes, but she's a fire hazard," she replied! "If there was a fire, she couldn't get out."

"I can assure you, if there was a fire or any other emergency, my wife would be the first one out of here!" Eddie said with a cheeky smile.

"I'm sorry, but she can't go in, maybe she would like to see the film with the children?"

"This is ridiculous!" I said, "Do you mean I can only watch the films showing on the ground floor?"

"I'm sorry but rules are rules, I can't allow you to see the Bruce Lee film."

I was embarrassed, I'd never been called a fire hazard before, many other names but never, "She's a fire hazard." Our day was ruined! Of course none of us could go in, I felt bad that it was because of me that the boys couldn't get into see the movie, but it wasn't my fault!

As we drove home, I began to get more and more angry, the injustice of the whole situation really got to me. The first thing I did was open the local paper to find the phone number of the cinema. Along with an advert boasting of their ten cinemas was the words 'WHEELCHAIR FRIENDLY" Huh! Now I was really fired up!

I phoned the cinema and asked to speak to the manager, it was obvious he was prepared and had been briefed about the situation before I spoke to him.

"I'm phoning to complain about being turned away from your cinema this evening."

"I am sorry, we are a wheelchair friendly cinema, you were welcome to see any film showing on the ground floor level."

"I wanted to see the Bruce Lee film!"

"We do our best to accommodate wheelchairs, but the city council have rules about public buildings and we have to comply with them."

"Who makes the rules, do they have a disabled person on the board to advise them?"

"I don't know, we have to abide by the rules."

It was obvious the conversation was going nowhere, so I left him with some food for thought;

"You obviously spend a lot of money advertising, would it be possible to put a wheelchair symbol beside the films disabled people can see, after all, there are 10 cinemas to choose from, it would save people travelling all the way to be humiliated and disappointed! I have been to the cinema many times, even during the 70's when there were bomb scares, when I was politely refused, but I have never been treated so badly in my whole life."

Later on that week, we all arrived at our local cinema, The Strand, on the Holywood Road where we had no problem at all. The staff were very courteous and helpful. My faith was restored!

Unfortunately, three years later, things are as bad as ever. Recently, there was a report in the local paper about a group of disabled people who were turned away from the same cinema!

CHAPTER SIXTEEN

The Thalidomide Action Group

Shortly before Christmas, 1993, I was having a leisurely morning sitting in my living room reading a book. I had the television on, but I wasn't really watching, as I sometimes simply have it switched on for 'background'. My ears pricked up at the mention of the word 'thalidomide'. I quickly lost interest in the book as I put it down to listen to what the presenter was saying. The programme was 'This Morning with Richard and Judy'. Appearing on the programme were two guys from Liverpool, they had started a campaign against Guinness PLC, the company who now owned Distillers, who had marketed thalidomide in the 60's.

The two guys went on to explain their aim was to look at the possibility of reopening the case. I watched in awe as they went on to speak about the tax situation regarding the money allocated to thalidomide victims.

"Good for you! It's time someone said something!" I shouted at the television!

As they outlined their case, they told the presenter that if Guinness were not prepared to meet them to discuss their concerns, they were planning to go on hunger-strike to highlight their plight, they seemed adamant that a hunger-strike was inevitable if Guinness ignored their request!

Although I sat full of admiration for the two guys, I was shocked to imagine they would really be prepared to go through with a hunger-strike as they had threatened.

However, on Christmas Eve 1993, Freddie Astbury, one of the guys interviewed, did just that! At the time I was under the impression that the guys were talking of an independent campaign, for the two of them personally, I didn't realise they were in fact campaigning for every thalidomide victim in Britain!

A few weeks later, I received a letter in the early morning post. When I opened it, I was surprised to see a questionnaire from Freddie, with a letter requesting me to fill in the form and add how I felt about the campaign against Guinness. I was really impressed with his dedication, so I decided to phone him instead!

I phoned his home, I wanted to tell him how much I admired him and also wish him the very best of luck.

"If there is anything I can do to help, just let me know," I offered.

Freddie explained in some detail exactly what he hoped to achieve by making the campaign known to as many people as possible.

"What you need is a woman to help in your campaign, preferably someone with kids! The media would show more interest in someone like that," I suggested.

We talked a little more and I wished him all the best again.

A few days later, the phone rang, it was Freddie.

"Kim, would you be interested in becoming involved in the campaign?"

"Me? I can't see what use I would be, living in Northern Ireland instead of the mainland, how could we work together living so far apart?"

Freddie said he was sure we could sort things out, and after some thought, I said I would help if I could.

When I replaced the receiver of the phone, I began to think to myself.

"What have I let myself in for?"

I had no experience of campaigning, the more I thought about it, the more frightened I became! What would Freddie expect of me? How would I deal with the media? My mind was whirling, just what extent of 'involvement' could I cope with? I didn't sleep much that night, nor the next few nights either!

Getting the media interested in me wasn't a problem as Freddie dealt with that end of things! Speaking to the newspapers became surprisingly easy for me. I felt at ease with their questions and was quietly confident with my answers.

My first television interview was something else altogether! I was asked by the local television station to do a live interview! I was a nervous wreck! I knew a lot of effort had been put into the campaign already and I didn't want to let anyone down. When the interview started, my confidence completely vanished, leaving me feeling adrift in a strange world I knew little or nothing about!

As I answered the questions fired at me by the interviewer, I was aware of my voice shaking with nerves! I felt completely intimidated by the interviewer. He was so professional and confident. One question he asked me, I had no answer for, so I gave what I felt was a ridiculous answer. I was also wary of the fact that the interviewer himself had a disabled child. Instead of feeling comfortable with the fact, I convinced myself that he was looking at me in a way that said,

"What right have you to campaign for more money, when my child has no special income?"

I wanted to say to him that there was a difference, his child was born disabled through nature, my circumstances were different. I was born because my mother had taken two tablets distributed by a multi-million pound company. But of course I said nothing, somehow I knew my thoughts were all jumbled up.

It was a nightmare! I was downhearted and felt I had only served to make a fool of myself and no good would come of my pathetic attempt to help Freddie and the others in the thalidomide group.

My family and friends all said the interview had gone really well, but I didn't feel happy with it at all. When I had calmed down I realised that my feelings about the interview had all been in my imagination! Completely irrational. Brought on by nervousness. I would have to be much better prepared next time!

I had a second interview shortly afterwards with the same guy, he greeted me like an old friend and he put me at my ease straight away. Any thoughts I previously had about him were quickly dispelled and I felt ashamed that I had even allowed myself to think in such a way!

In February 1994, an annual meeting of the Thalidomide Society took place at Runcorn Inn in Liverpool. I was unable to attend. During the meeting Freddie distributed membership forms to everyone interested in joining the Thalidomide Action Group. A girl called Heather Bird from Scotland joined on the spot! She was willing to fully participate and represent the victims from Scotland. Freddie was already representing England and Wales.

Now the whole of the United Kingdom was represented, Freddie would deal with the English members, Heather the Scottish and I would represent Northern Irish members. We made a joint decision to take some drastic measure to highlight the situation, we couldn't decide what though. A hunger strike was suggested, but I was dead against it!

"It's too serious to consider, once a hunger-strike is initiated, it would mean total commitment to the bitter end. Who would seriously be prepared to do that?"

As it happened, the matter was taken out of our hands when Heather told Freddie that she would go on hunger-strike! I had never met Heather at this stage, but Freddie told me she was a very determined character, she meant to go on strike, no matter what anyone else was doing! She told Freddie there was no other option and she would start her strike on February 23rd.

When Freddie phoned me with the news about Heather's decision, I asked for her phone number, I had to talk to this girl! When I had finished talking to Heather, I had made her a promise, I would go on hunger-strike in full support on February 28th!

"If you're determined to go on a hunger-strike, then I'll take the same action as you, we'll do it together!" I promised.

I felt it was the least I could do as Freddie and I were the Heads of the Action Group. Heather had only joined our group a few days previously now here she was prepared to take such drastic action to highlight our campaign!

When Heather began her hunger-strike, I phoned her as often as I could to see how she was doing, and of course offer her moral support, I admired her spirit and she was a strong character! The local media in Scotland were covering her action and I was busy psyching myself up for the ordeal I knew I would have to face.

I was a little disappointed to learn that the local television station had declined to cover the story of my impending hunger-strike. A girl I had gone to school with who worked for the station told me they felt it would be too much like encouraging me to go ahead with the strike. Well if they wouldn't cover the story, it would make no difference to my decision, whatever they thought! I had my mind made up, Heather had already started five days previously, now it was my turn!

I was to have my last meal at 12 o'clock noon on 28th February. Mum had arranged to have all my favourite food ready for me at her house. Just as I was about to leave the house, the phone rang. It was a reporter from Ulster Television asking if I would allow them to come and take some pictures, they had decided to cover the story after all! I was a little hesitant, I wasn't prepared at all for photographers! I had no make up on, my hair was a mess, and I was wearing an old T-shirt and leggings!

"I'm just on my way over to my Mum's house for my last meal, I don't know how my Mum will take it if there is a film crew all over the place!" I said feebly.

They liked the idea of my Mum having my 'last meal' prepared for me so they arranged to meet me at my Mum's house.

When I arrived at Mum's, she had a wonderful spread of food laid out on the table!

Before I could lift a single thing, the film crew arrived! They set up for filming and they wanted so many shots I thought I was never going to get stuck into the fantastic spread Mum had lovingly prepared for me! Just as I thought the film crew had shot enough footage, the Grandmother clock in Mum's hall struck 12 noon! It was too late to eat anything now, already I was starving! I couldn't change the plan to suit myself, it wouldn't be right, so I didn't eat my banquet. The film crew enjoyed it though!

The next day, the papers reported my action in full! Soon the phone was ringing almost continually, radio stations and various papers all wanted to know how I was feeling and if they could have an interview. Although my main reason for going on strike was to highlight our campaign, I also told the papers how disgusted I was at the fact that there were still thalidomide children being born in places like Brazil!

The papers carried many versions of my story, some of them had researched back to the 60's of find out details of the original Distillers publicity in relation to what became known as the Thalidomide Scandal. Whatever the outcome of my fast, the media were really helping to publicise our campaign.

DIARY OF MY HUNGER-STRIKE

DAY ONE: The phone keeps ringing! Press, media, and radio from all over Britain. Lots of calls from well-wishers. The food that I was supposed to eat I brought home for the kids. Mum's famous home-made scones I hadn't time to eat! Eddie came home and made the dinner. He told me that morning not to bother cooking anything for him. He said he would cook tonight, I suppose he thinks it would be cruel to expect me to cook!

DAY TWO: Too busy to think about food! Everyone wanted to interview me. I can't ever remember drinking so much tea, one cup after another all day long! The media have been so kind and thoughtful about the whole thing.

DAY THREE: My usual daily routine has to continue. I don't want to show the kids any sign of despair. I can see they are getting anxious about me not eating. Allan brought food into the living room and jokingly waved it about under my nose! Eddie cooked again for the third night in a row. He was thoughtful enough to close the kitchen door and living room door so I wouldn't have to smell the food! Today has been the hardest so far. I was experiencing hunger pains, I could murder a big mac!

Heather and I were on the phone at least five times today giving each other moral support and comparing 'ailments' a strange weakness came over me for a whole. At various stages I feel weak and then, all fired up. I get a surge of strength. One thing's for sure, I'm determined to stick it out!

The papers reported concern for Heather's health, she's been on strike for five days longer than me and has more physical and internal disabilities than me, I'm worried about her, so I phoned her even more! She's determined to continue whatever happens!

When I feel weak, I remember the pictures I saw on Yorkshire Television of the new generation of Thalidomide children and my determination soars, I have to keep going, the injustice of it is eating me up and keeping me fighting! While I'm at home, I'm reading everything I can get my hands on about the Thalidomide case. My hunger for knowledge and the history of my being born is all-consuming. I am appalled to read of the injustice my parents and other parents have been subjected to!

The more I read the more I felt justified in my actions, some people said we should:

"Forget about it and get on with our lives, it's history, it happened years ago, no-one cares about Thalidomide any more."

Even some fellow sufferers are against our actions. One guy went so far as to say to me that if we did ever get any compensation he would be looking for his share even though he thinks our actions were degrading!

"You have no right to tell everyone our private business, leave things alone!" he insisted.

"So if we succeed in getting compensation you won't want anything to do with it?"

"Oh yes, I will be looking for my fair share of whatever is awarded, I'm entitled to the same as anyone else!"

My faith in human nature is being tested to the limits! But luckily there are more positive people who go out of their way to tell me how much they support my stand for action!

I know from numerous phone calls that I have overwhelming support from the majority of people. Many of my fellow victims are living on very low incomes and are unable to work because of their disabilities. Took the phone off the hook for a while, it never stops! Went to bed early to get today over with!

DAY FOUR: Things seem better today, the hunger pains seem to have gone, but I feel so tired all the time, still a lot of media interest. Heather and Freddie both phoned today, they are concerned about me. They both say I'm too skinny anyway and I don't have much beef to keep me going! I was 5 stone 7 pounds when I started, I wonder what I will weigh when it's all over?

DAY FIVE: I was sick this morning, Yuk! being sick on an empty stomach was horrible! I feel so tired and weak. I lay down most of the day, but I have to leave for the airport soon as I have been asked to appear on a television show made by Central Weekend. Met Heather for the first time, it was good to finally meet the girl I had spent so much time speaking to over the phone! Freddie is also appearing, we were all nervous as the show is to go out live! There was an MP there, who insisted the Government has no responsibility, and a real brute of a young doctor! There were two women also appearing, one told the story of how she had been dependent on valium for 25 years, it broke my heart to hear her, and I was deeply offended when the young doctor said;

"O come off it! You're not trying to tell us that a few tablets destroyed your whole life!"

"How dare you! How dare you say that a few tablets can't ruin someone's life! Some of us here tonight can't do some simple things like play with our children ..."

My voice trailed off as I became very emotional and couldn't trust myself to say any more. The ignorance of the young doctor really brought me to boiling point!

"Where were you when I was taking valium? In nappies no doubt!" the woman shouted to him.

The audience applauded the woman wildly and the doctor had no reply for her.

His role was to defend the medical profession and the prescribing of any drugs by GPs. After the show, Freddie, Heather and myself were leaving the building when we saw the doctor again, he couldn't look at us and made a hasty exit! We later found out that he was a regular guest on the show and was well known for involving the audience and the other guests in heated exchanges! I reckoned he had a lucky escape as Heather was revving up the electric wheelchair to run him over! In the time I spent talking to Heather, I was sure she would have no hesitation in doing it, and she would have reversed over him to make sure she'd done the job right! I like Heather! Went back to our Hotel, stayed up talking for ages with Heather and Freddie, I'm absolutely exhausted and I miss the kids.

DAY SIX: Flew back from Birmingham, the airport staff congratulated me on the show. Glad to be home! It's amazing! I don't feel hungry at all. Still tired and still weak. It's as if everything is happening in slow motion. I received a disturbing phone call from a man in his early 50's, who lives in Northern Ireland. He phoned the local News Letter paper and asked them for my phone number. He told me that for the past 8 weeks he has been taking a drug called 'sauramide' for severe mouth ulcers. He says his doctor told him he would be safe to take the drug as the only side effect was on the foetus of an unborn baby. His doctor said the drug was actually Thalidomide! The man said he was experiencing numbness in his fingertips and toes. He asked me if it was possible for Thalidomide to have any other side effects. He wanted to be sure if he was having symptoms due to the drug he was on. He sounds really frightened.

I phoned a friend who quoted me a section from a book written in 1968 called 'The Body' by Anthony Smith. It confirms that the symptoms described to me by the caller are indeed a side effect of prolonged use of Thalidomide. It brings on a form of neuritis! I phoned the man back as promised with the news, he was devastated and said he would stop taking them immediately! He asked me to give him an honest answer, was the damage permanent? I told him prolonged use could make the damage irreversible. I felt so sorry for him, I was

sickened and horrified today! This drug is still ruining people's lives!!
I am more determined than ever to go ahead with my action!

DAY SEVEN: Still all of the above I feel light-headed and so
ill. Very, very tired. Depression reared its ugly head! I seem to be
hurting my family so much. But I have to go on, I can't fail!

DAY EIGHT: Today is bad, I can't give in. I have to continue.
I feel no sign of weakness mentally. I can't let everyone down, so
much depends on the success of the hunger strike. I feel dizzy, dou-
ble-vision. I had to lie down on the floor and I watched the room
spin. The media came to interview me, I'm off to London tonight. I
piled the make-up on to cover my pale complexion and put on a
confident happy expression. I didn't want anyone to see how much
pain I felt. One interviewer commented how terrific I look throughout it all!!

DAY NINE: I was up until 2 o'clock this morning. Freddie
came to the hotel to make final arrangements for tomorrow. We went
over our statements we planned to give to the press, we wanted it all
to go like clockwork. Up again at 5 o'clock to appear on GMTV at
6.30 lack of sleep didn't help at all, I still feel drained and weak.

While I was in London, I met quite a few celebrities. After the
interview with GMTV, Mr Motivator, the resident fitness instructor
spoke to me. I asked him why he didn't do any exercises for disabled
people.

"O but I do! You mustn't be up early enough in the morning!"
he answered!

"Sorry, I'll have to make a point of getting up to watch you, I
could do with some tummy exercises myself!!"

"I'm due to go on air soon, why don't you come with me and
we'll do some exercise together?"

I politely refused, I was still weak and I didn't think I could lift
a finger let alone my tummy muscles!

The next day, I was to appear on a talk show called 'Kilroy'.
The topic for discussion was, "Disabled people and their relation-
ships". I had received a phone call before the hunger strike as someone had put my name forward to the television company. I found out
later that it was a neighbour of mine who had phoned the company
about me!

The show was taped on Thursday, 10th march, the day after I came off the hunger strike. After the show finished Robert Kilroy-Silk came over to me.

"I was sitting last night going over the names of the guests due to appear on today's show, when I heard the name 'Kim Morton' on the national news! I had just reached the same name on my list. I couldn't believe it, what a coincidence!" he told me.

He was very friendly and charming, and I could only smile, it's not often I'm at a loss for words, or so I'm told!

On the day I went to Downing Street with Eddie, Heather, Freddie and my MP Peter Robinson, I had mixed feelings. Heather and I arrived at Number 10 and Heather handed a letter outlining our demands. There were four main concerns;

1. Adequate compensation for the victims of Thalidomide.

2. A public inquiry into the tragedy.

3. Stricter controls on the continued use and distribution of the drug.

4. Tax of 35% abolished or at least reduced on income from the trust fund.

I hoped things would go well, but I was dreading what might be waiting for us. What if the meeting went badly? I had vowed to continue my hunger strike until some of our demands were met, the media had reported my every word, and I had meant every word, I was willing to starve to death if our demands were not met! As I entered the meeting I was acutely aware that my whole future lay in what was about to happen, I had no control now, it was out of my hands!

When we emerged from the meeting, the press were waiting for a statement. Things had gone fairly well, the Government had promised to look into our demands and we had created a lot of interest in our case. It was time to end the strike, we were all agreed. As I said earlier in my story, Peter Robinson spoke to me about my family's anxiety especially my Mum's. I personally felt we had achieved all we could for the time being. Any campaign plan would be best served by keeping ourselves strong and well informed. I began to read everything I could find about Thalidomide, Distillers, and Guinness.

My first night at home after the hunger strike was called off, I couldn't sleep at all! I kept rolling things over in my mind. So many different emotions were sweeping over me. On the one hand, I felt justified in the campaign, on the other I felt guilty. Had I been wrong to do what I had done? What had I started? Was I doing the right thing? How would my family react to my busy schedule now I was a very active member and I had committed myself so fully in the campaign? As I drifted into a fitful sleep, I prayed to God to give me some sign that I was doing the right thing, and to give me strength and guidance.

Apart from visits to England to see their Dad, Allan, Russell and Marc had never been away from me at all. Going to their Dad was very different from me being away. Being at home without their Mum appeared to make them feel uneasy. When Eddie and I arrived home, they were very inquisitive and clingy, I hated to be away from them and I ran up a dreadful phone bill phoning as often as I could!

Frances had been minding the kids for me, and I knew it was difficult for her as she had a young baby of her own, but my family was behind me all the way, and they all knew I was determined to carry through my decision to campaign for the Thalidomide Action Group. If I was to carry on campaigning I was going to need as much help as I could get from everyone, and I knew I only had to ask, but I didn't want to burden anyone too much.

On the Friday morning, as a treat for the kids, I phoned their schools and asked if it would be possible for them to have the day off school. I really felt I needed to spend some time with them, and they seemed to have been through a lot of worry while I had been on strike. With so much going on over the last two weeks, I really hadn't given them any attention worth mentioning! The headmaster at Russell's school asked if it would be possible for me to call and see him later on in the afternoon. I said I would call in to see him.

We all got ready, but Eddie had to go back to work, he had used up all his days owed to him so it was just the boys and myself. We left to go out for lunch at a local restaurant 'The Queen's Inn'. The kids were full of chatter and were obviously enjoying their day out and having me all to themselves. Marc had so many questions about my visit to London, and Russell and Allan wanted to know what the television personalities had said to me. I didn't have much of an appetite yet, but I wanted the boys to enjoy their meal.

"Order whatever you want, and you can have two desserts if you want!" I declared.

"Brilliant!" they said in unison.

Just as we were ordering our meal, the owner of the restaurant came over to our table.

"Congratulations on your campaign. I have been following your story on the news! Please order whatever you want, it's on the house! By the way if you are looking for a venue for a charity night for those little children in Brazil just let me know and I will organise a night here for you!" he offered.

"Thank you very much! I might just take you up on your offer, thank you!" I replied. The boys' eyes lit up.

"Can we order more cappuccinos Mum?"

"Yes I said you can have whatever you want and I meant it!"

We had a great family day together and I really needed the time with the boys, they'd been so good throughout everything! When it came time to pay our bill the receptionist said it was taken care of, it was a lovely gesture!

We arrived home full of laughter and the boys were in great form joking and larking about! We were only in the house a few minutes when the phone rang. It was a researcher from the BBC to ask if I would be available to appear on a local talk show called 'Anderson on the Box'.

"When would you want me to be there?" I enquired.

"Tonight, the show is going out live and we want to speak to you as it's Mothering Sunday this weekend and we would really like to hear bout your campaign."

"Tonight! I don't know, it's very short notice!"

"You'll be fine, we'll organise everything, don't worry about a thing" she assured me.

I said I would be there and we made arrangements for Eddie, the boys and myself to go to the BBC studios later that same evening.

With all the excitement I nearly forgot about Russell's Head-master! When I arrived at the school, I was shown into the office.

"I'm concerned about Russell, his choice of Secondary schools appears to be a little rash" he said.

"I think he's worried about the travelling to and from school, someone told him he has to get 4 buses to Wellington College! That seems a bit extreme" I explained.

"Well 4 buses is certainly excessive, if you think Russell really wants to attend Wellington College, I will speak to him and try to allay his fears, he's a very bright boy, and I believe he could do well at Wellington."

I left the school and spoke to Russell, he did want to go to Wellington, but was put off at the thought of not getting home until late. We agreed he would attend for 6 months to see how things worked out. It was a good feeling to sort out a nice simple family problem for a change! I felt like 'Mum' again, I hadn't felt so simplistic in ages!

No sooner had I sorted out that problem than another one arose. Who could take me to the ladies while I was at the BBC studio? I phoned Beatrice!

"Get your gladrags on, and come out with me tonight, I'm go-ing to be on Anderson on the Box!"

"Pull the other one! When did this happen? "I'm telling you, I have to be at the studios tonight and I need you to go to help me if I need to go to the ladies Will you come?"

"Well I'm standing here in my scruffs as I had a previous en-gagement with a pile of ironing ... O all right then, you don't have to beg" she teased.

We arranged to meet at the car park. When we arrived the re-searcher welcomed us and showed us into the 'Green Room'. Beatrice was pushing me in the wheelchair, as we entered the room I nearly died of shock when I saw a row of Teddy-boys wearing fluorescent pink and green socks sitting at the far end of the room! For a fleeting moment I dreamed they were my teenage idols SHOWADDY-WADDY!!

"Beatrice!! There's Showaddywaddy!" I said though trying to keep my voice low so no-one could hear me!

"Bring me over beside them quick!" I begged her! I couldn't believe my luck!

As I got closer, I realised they were indeed Showaddywaddy! I was so excited. Eddie gave me a look as if to say;

"Calm down Kim"

I gave Eddie a look that said;

"Leave me alone, I'm loving every minute!"

Beatrice pushed me over beside the group of 'Teddy-boys'. Just as I was thinking of something to start a conversation with Dave Bartram, (who I had worshipped as a teenager) Romeo, another member of the group looked straight at me and said in a deep rich voice;

"Hey, I was lying in bed yesterday morning when I saw you on my T.V. didn't I? Were you on hunger strike or something."

"Yes, it was me!" I answered feeling really chuffed to think that a member of my favourite group had seen ME on television!!

We talked for a while, and I said to Romeo;

"I used to be madly in love with Dave Bartram when I was younger!"

Dave Bartram obviously overheard as he looked at me and smiled, blushing almost as much as I was when I realised he had heard what I had said about him!

During the show, Gerry Anderson, the host, asked me how I was feeling and also asked Marc and Allan what they intended to do for Mother's Day. They were thrilled to be on T.V. As a complete surprise I was given tickets for a family weekend in a luxury hotel in Newcastle, a beautiful scenic town where the 'Mountains of Mourne sweep down to the sea' to quote a famous song.

I had earlier turned down payment for my interview requesting a donation for the 'Brazilian Children Fund', but Gerry Anderson gave me a beautiful bouquet of flowers in the 'Green Room' later on, and explained that the BBC wanted to give me something for myself and I deserved a break after what I had been through. I had a thoroughly enjoyable but exhausting day!

The weekend thankfully was relatively quiet, apart from phone calls from family and friends wanting to hear how I was doing. The phone rang a lot during the campaign, so I had recently bought an answering machine.

However, on the Sunday evening I was relaxing with Eddie and the boys when I had a phone call from a woman I can only describe as sick. When I lifted the receiver I heard a rasping voice;

"You're dead Kim Morton! I'm going to kill you!"

I put the phone down and shrugged my shoulders, I wasn't going to let some crank upset me so I laughed it off. However, the next day the phone rang again.

"You're really dead now" the voice said.

"Is that all you phoned to say? I'm busy vacuuming at the minute, I've better things to do with my time, unlike you obviously" I answered getting irritated more by the nuisance of answering the phone!

I told Eddie about the phone calls and he had the same attitude as I had. It was just some crank who had read my story in the papers and felt the need to try to scare me! Later the same day, the phone rang again. This time Allan answered.

"Tell you Mum she's dead, do you hear me? DEAD!" the woman's voice growled at Allan.

"Mum! Some woman said she's going to kill you! Who is it Mum? Why does someone want to kill you Mummy?"

That was it! I wasn't going to let this woman upset my children, it was bad enough calling me and threatening me, but my son! I simply couldn't let it go on! I took the phone from Allan and held it to my ear while she ranted and raved on about what she was going to do to me.

"A slow death!" were her last words she spoke before I interrupted her.

"Wise up and get a life!" I said as calmly as I could.

That night, all I could think of was the look of fear on Allan's face, he was visibly shaken after listening to the ramblings of the mystery woman, he kept asking me who she was. I didn't know who it was, but whoever it was wouldn't get the opportunity to put any child of mine through an ordeal like that again!

I phoned the police. They were very helpful and arranged for British Telecom to monitor my calls. They kept in touch with me every week for the next three months, but she never phoned back.

Perhaps she was a mother herself, and Allan lifting the phone pricked her conscience, I don't know, but I feel sorry for someone who feels compelled to do something so sordid to a complete stranger.

I later heard from Freddie that he had received a threatening phone call and Heather had received 2 calls but neither of them had let it bother them too much!

The next thing I planned to do was to concentrate on the appeal for the Brazilian children. I had already had some donations from neighbours and friends, and it seemed everywhere I went someone asked me if there was anything they could do to help raise money for the new generation of Thalidomide children in Brazil.

Ever since I watched the documentary made by Yorkshire Television, I had been unable to get the vision of those unfortunate children out of my mind. Even after the tragedy in the 60's with Thalidomide, here we were in the 90's and little babies were still being born with horrendous deformities! I have to admit I was angry!

I thought it best to use my anger and transform it into some useful energy. I began to research into the background of how the drug had been made available to the Brazilian people in such a way. It appeared Leprosy was a major problem there and the drug containing Thalidomide was successful in helping people with the disease.

I spoke to Freddie and he said he would find out as much as he could by contacting the documentary team on Yorkshire Television. Freddie put me in contact with one researcher who was extremely helpful, he sent full colour photographs of the children featured on the programme, along with a full transcript.

I found out that 30 children had been born Thalidomide, the drug was freely available.

I shed a few tears while reading the case histories of the new generation Brazilian victims of Thalidomide, and I really wanted to do something to help. Freddie arranged for the 2 of us to have a visit with someone from the Brazilian Embassy. The meeting was to take place in May, meanwhile I started trying to organise some fund-raising.

A neighbour and good friend of mine owned a popular night-spot in the centre of Belfast. She offered to hold a charity night to help raise funds for the Brazilian children. The tickets sold really well and I managed to get a few local celebrities to appear in cabaret. It was a good start to the appeal. The manager of my local restaurant who had kindly offered to hold a charity night also arranged a night which proved successful. The Beechlawn Hotel, The Cosy Bar and Caz's fish and chip shop, all local businesses held appeals and in total the fund eventually reached £1950!

CHAPTER SEVENTEEN

Standing ovation

On March 14th, I received a letter from Councillor Reverend Eric Smyth of Belfast City Council. In the letter he said he had followed the campaign on television and he wanted to offer his help in any way he could. He asked if I would permit him to put a motion forward to the Belfast City Council to support our claim for adequate compensation for the British Thalidomide victims. A few days later, I received a phone call from a dear family friend. It was Reverend Harvey!

"Dearest Kim, I just wanted to tell you how much I admire your stand and to tell you how brave I think you are. I feel very honoured to know you and I want to wish you and your fellow sufferers every success in your campaign!" he said.

To hear Reverend Harvey's words of encouragement meant a great deal to me! I thanked him for taking time to call, and he said he would be following the campaign with great interest. To receive the letter from Councillor Reverend Eric Smyth as well, seemed to be an answer to my prayers, or was it just coincidence? Whatever the interpretation, I was moved to continue my fight for justice.

I phoned Reverend Smyth to thank him for his kind letter, and his offer to put forward a motion for our group. He explained he would bring the matter up at the next council meeting, and he would look into the possibility of allowing myself and 2 others into the council chambers instead of the public gallery.

I later received a letter confirming the date for the council meeting where the motion would be put forward. On April 5th I left the house with Eddie to attend the meeting. I asked 2 fellow group members to attend with me and we met them at City Hall that evening.

We were greeted by Reverend Smyth and I was impressed by his genuine desire to help our cause. He had a witty sense of humour and put us at our ease immediately. As we were shown into the council chambers I felt apprehensive to say the least! An array of faces greeted me, faces I had often seen on local television, but didn't realise just how formal and grand the occasion was going to be!

The chambers were beautiful! The benches were beautifully carved and each bench had a row of individual microphones. The atmosphere was electric and I was in awe as I looked around at the chambers where so many years of history were entrenched.

We were shown to our seats, where the Lord Mayor Reg Empey was seated to our left. Reverend Smyth put the motion forward and was seconded by the High Sheriff, Margaret Crooks. As Reverend Smyth explained why the motion should be passed, each representative of their political party took it in turns to speak. Together in the chambers were the Democratic Unionists, Social Democratic Labour Party, the Alliance Party, Ulster Unionists, and Sinn Fein as well as independent representatives from other parties.

I was overwhelmed as every single speaker voiced their approval and support for the campaign.

"Can we take this a stage further and invite the Managing Director of Guinness to the Belfast City Council to have talks about the fears Kim and her group have" said one Councillor.

"It would be an idea to invite Baroness Denton to the chambers to hear what Kim has to say" said another.

As I sat listening to the various councillors I couldn't believe they were talking about me! I hadn't until that moment realised just how much impact the campaign had obviously had on the public. It was also a revelation to me to hear councillors from both sides of the political divide actually agreeing on something! Each and every spokesperson spoke highly about my stand for Thalidomide victims.

The motion was passed unanimously! I was dumbfounded as the councillors rose to their feet and began to applaud rapturously! As the tears welled in my eyes I mouthed the words 'Thank You'. I felt so emotional I could hardly lift my head. I felt very humble as I looked towards Eddie. His face beamed with pride as he looked at me, I was on a high as the adrenalin pulsed through my body, it was one of the best nights of my life.

We were invited to the Lord Mayor's parlour for refreshments to meet the councillors. By the time we arrived, I had composed myself and was able to thank them individually for their support. One councillor congratulated me on making history.

"I believe you have made history tonight! As far as I am aware there has never been such a huge vote with a unanimous decision!" he said.

When we arrived back home my 2 fellow members Tony and Janet, Eddie and I talked for ages about the evening. We were all ecstatic by the outcome. It was the early hours of the morning before I could settle down to sleep.

I began to devote every minute I could spare to the Action Group, and the Appeal. Meanwhile, Eddie had commented a few times about his workplace. Since Christmas the yard where he worked had seemed so very slack, and lately things appeared worse. The trailers which usually filled the yard were few and far between, and there was talk of redundancies, so Eddie reckoned it was only a matter of time before the firm closed down. Soon, his fears were confirmed, they were looking for 4 volunteers for redundancy.

We talked at some length about Eddie accepting redundancy, and we weighed up the pros and cons. We talked about it generally at first, and then decided it was a definite option. With my regular trips back and forward to London, the kids were having to endure a lot of to-ing and fro-ing to my sister Frances' and Mum's homes. I hated the thought of them having to leave their own home every time! I knew they were being well cared for, but the conversation between Eddie and I always seemed to involve the fact that the boys had to be unsettled every time I went away.

With Eddie at home, it would mean that the boys could stay in their own home and regain the stability they had been used to. Eddie was also a great cook, so he could look after that end of things! We decided it would be best for everyone if Eddie accepted the redundancy. Besides, Eddie was convinced the firm was going to close eventually anyway. First thing Monday morning he put his name forward.

We didn't realise how fast everything would happen! That Thursday Eddie finished work and received his redundancy payment. We haven't regretted our decision as things have worked out very well. Eddie hasn't travelled to London since, as he stays at home to look after the boys and everyone is happy with the situation.

On the same day Eddie finished work, I was due to attend an award ceremony at Castlereagh Borough Council. I had previously received a letter telling me I had been nominated for an award as 'a high achiever'. The letter was from Tommy Jeffers, the Mayor of Castlereagh, and as I read on I became very nervous. I felt honoured at the prospect of receiving such an award.

People from all walks of life, who had at one time lived in Castlereagh were invited to receive awards. They included Ray Close, the boxer; Peter Corry, an entertainer and others including gifted children. As my name was called out and the reason for my nomination given, Eddie wheeled me to the front of the hall to be presented with my plaque. I had promised to give a speech, but when the moment arrived I was speechless! Many of the audience who knew me laughed at my silence as they knew I was a chatterbox! In the end, I mumbled;

"Thank you, just ... thank you!"

As a complete surprise, Peter Robinson, my MP, received a special award also, for his work in the community. I was delighted to be there to see him receive his plaque, as I was deeply indebted to him for his help and dedicated hard work during the campaign, especially while I was in London. His continuing interest in the Thalidomide Action Group has not diminished one bit since the hunger-strike.

One afternoon as I was getting ready to pick Marc up from school, I answered the phone to an English newspaper reporter. She explained that he paper had covered the story of the campaign. She said the paper had received a letter addressed to me from a woman who desperately wanted to contact me. The reporter asked if I would mind giving them my address so they could forward the letter on.

I gave he my address and left to pick Marc up. I had received many letters from people all over the British Isles. One autograph hunter, who had made a hobby of collection famous peoples' autographs wrote to me enclosing a copy of a magazine article charting his quest for autographs. He penned a very pleasant letter assuring me he was genuine. I felt very strange autographing a photograph of myself as he had requested, and Eddie teased me mercilessly about it!

I also received a postcard from an artist offering to donate one of his original paintings to raise money for the Brazilian children. At the time I was very busy and I lost the address, I was very sad to lose the card as it depicted a shire horse, in a beautiful setting hand-painted by the artist, I had every intention of writing back thanking him, but I lost his address! I had so many letters, I found it impossible to answer every one. I wrote to as many people as I could, but unfortunately some very genuine and caring people never received a reply from me, I still feel sad when I think about that. However, I was so moved by the letter I received from the woman in England who had written to me via the newspaper, I contacted her immediately.

Here is the full content of her letter to me.

Dear Kim Morton,

I am writing to you as I saw you in our local Echo, about you trying to get compensation for Thalidomide. I have been trying to get compensation for the last thirty years, as the doctor I had at the time gave me Thalidomide and

I had a letter from Lady Somebody (I can't remember her name) saying she was sorry to hear I had a Thalidomide baby, and as I had gone almost full time with my son, I was entitled to compensation. I took the letter to the doctor so he would give me the information and he told me not to make trouble for him, otherwise he would make trouble for me. He refused to write down on my medical card that he'd given it to me. His words were (so I would not have proof) that he gave it to me. He used me as an illegal guinea pig and he and the drug company did not want anybody to know.

I've been trying to get him and the drug company to court ever since. I've been to see the local MP, solicitors and police. All say I have a good case until I tell them the doctor's name. Then their attitude changes and they say there is nothing they can do.

This doctor and the drug company killed my baby son and I can't get anybody to help me get them both to court. I am writing to ask if you know anybody to help me. This doctor, though I asked and requested a post mortem on my son to find out why my son was deformed. Instead of getting a post mortem do you know what he done? He burnt my son's body on my kitchen fire and he said we don't need no evidence about. I've been trying for thirty years to get them both to court, I need help as I've not been able to put my son to rest, and it's playing on my health. There's so much to tell I've been threatened that if I keep trying to make trouble I would be crossed off the medical list. I would not be covered by any doctor or hospital.

My son's legs, instead of being straight down like they should be, are growing above his head. Please, please, please can you help me?

I have suffered this torment for too long while this doctor and the drug company have got away with killing my son and they are laughing at me. My story would fill a

whole writing pad as there is lots more to my story.
Thank you for listening to me.

Yours faithfully,
Marion

As I held the letter in my hand I felt sick and horrified. There had been lots of rumours about Thalidomide babies being killed, there was even a court case in Belgium where a couple were charged with murdering their baby! But to read Marion's letter in such simple words brought a wave of emotion to me so strong, I was bewildered as to what I should do.

I knew instinctively that the letter was genuine. The 'lady' she had referred to was Lady Hoare, an aristocrat who had started a chain of charity clothes shops to help Thalidomide children in the late 60's. The picture Marion had drawn also hit a chord with me.

I remembered my father and mother telling me how I had looked when I was born. My legs were twisted upwards just as she had described her son's legs. In fact, her son looked chillingly similar to myself. My blood ran cold, my forehead was pulsating, there was such a cocktail of emotions going on in my head, I didn't know what to do for the best. Marion had typed her name, address and telephone number at the top of her letter, I lifted the phone to call her, but changed my mind. As soon as I put the receiver down, I lifted it again.

I dialled the number at the top of the page,
"Hello this is Kim Morton"
"O hello, I'm so glad you've phoned"
"Do you want to talk to me about your son?" I asked.

She started to tell me about the birth of her son. The baby had been born alive at her home, her mother-in-law was attending the birth. She had heard her baby cry and then … silence. She said she had asked her doctor what happened to her baby, but the doctor was very vague. He had told her the baby had been stillborn, but she heard him cry!

I told Marion I would contact someone and find out if there was anyone who could help her and I promised to keep in touch.

"It was so nice to talk to someone who understands, thank you for your time" she said.

I could hardly get the little drawing of her baby son out of my head. I did keep in touch with Marion and her letter is printed here with her full permission.

CHAPTER EIGHTEEN

Heartbreak and hope

On the day I received the letter from Marion, a film crew from BBC Scotland arrived at my house to make a documentary. It was a really hectic day! Mum had spent the whole morning baking and preparing a buffet for everyone. We knew there was going to be a lot of visitors and I had arranged for Heather and four other Thalidomide victims to visit. It was purely coincidental that the film crew was there the same day, but my house was buzzing all day long.

The furniture had to be moved out of the way so the crew could take shots around the house. Eddie moved the settee while I sat on the floor. The phone rang and as it had been moved out into the hall I got on to the settee as I always do, and jumped down off the back to get across to the phone, one of the crew members thought I had fallen off, so he jumped up,

"Are you all right?" he said with a concerned look on his face.

"Yes, I'm fine, would anyone like a cup of tea?"

"Cup of tea! You scared the wits out of me! I think I need a double scotch love! Don't you bother, I'll make the tea!" he offered.

He seemed to think I was incapable of making a cup of tea, but I soon assured him I was more than able! As the day progressed, I think I must have made a hundred cups of tea, we were awash with the stuff!

I had arranged a meeting for Action Group members and the BBC team asked if they could stay on and film our meeting. We all gathered in The Queen's Inn where there was a quiz night taking place, so when the formalities were taken care of, we all took part, and the atmosphere was relaxing and thoroughly enjoyable. The film crew joined in, and included some of the shots taken at the quiz in their documentary.

I received a copy of the finished documentary by the BBC and I personally felt the programme was very balanced and well re-searched. There was some archive footage showing very young Tha-lidomide children being fitted with monstrous robotic limbs. At the time the main objective was to make us look as 'normal' to the out-side world as possible.

As I watched one of the mass meetings held for the parents, one woman tore at my heart-strings as she spoke. As tears streamed down her face and her eyeliner ran blackening her cheeks, she sobbed as she explained to the reporter what was going on in the meeting.

"I've been told by my solicitor that if I don't accept one of these two settlements today, and if I talk to the press or television, I will have to find another solicitor!"

She was so distraught, she was inconsolable. As I looked around the sea of faces of the other parents on the screen, I was saddened to see the sheer despair and anguish etched on their faces. It was one of those meetings I had heard my mother and father speak about, where emotional blackmail was the order of the day. Parents were emotion-ally drained and battle-weary, how on earth could the system allow such blatant blackmail to take place I asked myself? It was 1970, when ordinary people were not so well aware of their rights, and they were taken full advantage of!

As I rewound the video, I phoned Freddie to tell him about watching the footage of the woman crying. As I described her to him he said,

"Kim that was my Mum". I knew Freddie's Mum had passed on, and somehow knowing who this woman really was made the film and the injustice of the settlement all the more poignant.

For the next few weeks, I had such a heavy schedule I thought I would never fit everything in. There was a meeting held with a representative from Guinness in City Hall. He had been invited by the Belfast City Council as promised. Unfortunately, the meeting proved fruitless, but later on, in the Lady Mayoress's parlour, I spoke to the representative. He was a pleasant man and he listened very intently. I felt from the look he gave me as he left, that if he had a million pounds in his pocket that day, he would have given it to us himself with a heart and a half!

As we were discussing how the meeting had gone with the Mayor and other councillors, a deafening explosion brought the talks to a sudden halt. We knew immediately it was a bomb, but we were unaware at the time it was actually the building we were in! The councillors disappeared and Margaret Crooks, the High Sheriff, ran in and said we would have to evacuate the building immediately! As I watched the news later at home, I heard that 2 workmen had been seriously hurt when they had been blown off scaffolding outside the City Hall.

That same week, I met Baroness Denton for the first time. She was the Minister for Health in Northern Ireland. I found her to be a very genuine concerned and understanding lady. She made a real impression on me and followed our meeting up with a three page letter, she was a lovely person, and I feel privileged to have met her.

Next on the agenda was for me to take part in the Mayor of Castlereagh's 'Mayorathon' I had been asked by the Mayor to participate in raising money for cancer research, and I was more than happy to oblige. The events began at 7 o'clock in the morning, the idea was to do as many activities as possible within a 12 hour period! PHEW! I hadn't been so physically active in years!

Obviously there were some activities I couldn't take an active part in, but when it came to the 'free-fall slide' in the Indianaland indoor adventure park, there was no stopping me!!!

However when I actually arrived at the top of the slide and realised it was a sheer drop, my courage left me for a moment. Allan, my eldest son, came to the rescue and showed me how 'easy' it was … twice, well I had to be sure it was safe didn't I? The longer I hesitated the more people gathered around to watch the spectacle, I could hardly compose myself as I started to giggle, (more to do with nerves than anything else).

When Allan did the 'drop', he held on to the bar above, while his feet anchored him until he was ready to release his grip. It proved impossible for me to do the same though, as my arms were too short to reach the bar and of course, I had no legs to anchor myself in readiness for the 'drop'!! Eddie came and lifted me and we tried various ways to find a safe way to drop me. There 'audience' were in hysterics as he lifted me this way, and that way, then hung me over the drop, then I lifted my bottom over the edge and nearly lost my grip on Eddie!! AAR-GH!

"Don't let go!! Don't let go!! I screamed at him!"

I knew Eddie wouldn't do anything to put me in danger, but it was a sheer drop and I'd never done anything like that before. Amidst the laughter and cheeky comments flying around from a few 'smart alecs' in the 'audience', we decided it would be best if Eddie held my wrists and dangled me over the precipice, with my rear-end just touching the top of the slide. Everyone seemed to hold their breath as Eddie let go of my wrists,,,,,,WHOOSH! I came to a halt in a split second as I was enveloped in a sea of brightly coloured plastic balls! WOW!

I laughed so much, I was helpless to extract myself out of the plastic balls, so the Mayor came over but he was laughing uncontrollably too! We soon stopped when the photographer told us that his shot of me had only captured the top of my head as the fall was so fast!

"Will you do it again?" he asked!

"Yes! it was brilliant, no problem!" I said as I climbed back up onto the platform. I was hooked!

At the end of an exhilarating day, quite a healthy amount was raised for cancer research, so it was well worth turning my hair white. (Most people think it's out of a bottle, but it was the shock of that drop! Promise!)

The publicity surrounding our campaign brought many, many phone calls. One was from a local radio station, they wanted me to go on air live to give them an update on what had been happening since the hunger-strike. On the morning I was due to go on air, I had a phone call from a fellow Thalidomide Group member. She was really pleased to tell me that she had been awarded Income Support.

At the time, we had been refused any support whatsoever, and I thought we had been dealt with unfairly. I phoned my local DHSS office to enquire if the law had recently been changed with regard to payments. When I was told it was still the same, I explained that I had applied for Income Support when I was separated, and I relayed the episode where the adjudication officer had come to my house and laughed in my face.

"O, there's been a girl in the news recently who's Thalidomide, are you like her?" the girl asked.

"Well actually I am her, I'm just about to go on the radio, and I just wanted to check because I desperately needed your help a couple of years ago, and you weren't there for me, so I will be telling people about the way I have been treated."

"I'll get back to you with someone in management to speak to you" she said.

Within 10 minutes, I had 2 phone calls from the office and I was promised a form would be sent out to me to claim back money, and an apology because I had been misinformed.

I went ahead with the radio interview, and the presenter and I had a very friendly chat. I thought it best to leave the issue with the DHSS until I received the letter.

The form arrived as promised, but at the time I was in the middle of finalising travel arrangements to London. Freddie had arranged a meeting at the Brazilian Embassy for us, as we wanted to talk about our concerns over the new Thalidomide children being born in their country. Freddie was a magician at opening doors for the Group! Wherever we needed to go, Freddie could always come up with a plan to get us there! No matter what was thrown at us from any quarter, he could always punch holes in their arguments with well researched facts and figures!

Eddie and I arrived in London and met Freddie and Heather outside the Embassy. We were greeted by the Ambassador's representative, who gave us a warm welcome. We explained our fears about the Thalidomide problem which was highlighted by the recent documentary on Yorkshire Television.

"We have not had a Thalidomide born in our country for 30 years" he declared.

We were well prepared for our visit, and I produced a large brown envelope from my briefcase, and handed him a thick pile of case histories of children who had been born within the last 10 years. Each colour photograph of a deformed child had the name, age and a brief description relating to the child typed underneath. The representative was clearly shocked as he looked at each page in turn.

"I don't know what to say to you, but I will need more proof than this, to show me the drug is actually being used in my country."

I reached into my handbag and pulled out a long tinfoil strip of tablets. As I handed it to him, he stared at it for what seemed to be an eternity. Heather, Freddie and I looked at each other, we could see the genuine shock on his face. At the time I hadn't realised that printed on the packaging was indisputable evidence that the 'Thalidomida' tablets I had produced were actually made by a pharmaceutical company owned by the Brazilian Government.

"Well, you can't get much more evidence than this!" he conceded.

He gave a short nervous laugh, it was clear to me that he had no idea that his country had anything to do with Thalidomide, and he had been shocked at our revelations.

What followed next I can only describe as an 'eerie' silence, I could almost see the wheels inside his head turning, I broke the silence.

"Can you tell me what action your Government is prepared to take to stop this going on?"

"What are you hoping to achieve from today's discussions?" he asked.

"The immediate withdrawal of Thalidomide from your country" I answered.

Freddie then spoke,

"We will give you a month, and we would then like it in writing that Thalidomide has been fully withdrawn from use in your country. If we don't receive an official letter from your Embassy stating that the drug has been withdrawn within that time, we plan to picket outside this Embassy until we do."

The representative gave us his word that we would hear from his Embassy within the month. The meeting ended amicably, and we spent more time than we planned to, so we missed an important meeting with our barrister. We headed straight to the airport to catch our plane. Freddie and Eddie and myself had tea at the airport and we were elated at what we could have achieved. If even one child was saved from being born Thalidomide, it would be a triumph!

Within 5 weeks of our meeting at the Embassy, Freddie phoned to tell me that he had received a letter from the Brazilian Ambassador. There was no misinterpretation of the letter, Thalidomide had been withdrawn from their country! I felt an overwhelming sense of achievement as I realised the enormity of what we had achieved. I retrieved the case histories of the Brazilian children and looked over them once more ...

"Please God, let them be the last!" I thought.

That night I prayed that the word 'Thalidomide' would never be used to describe a new-born baby.

I had one appointment to keep which made me feel a little uncomfortable. I had been nominated for a certificate of merit by the William Keown Trust. I knew that the awards were normally given to children of courage or people who had overcome extreme hardship and I didn't feel worthy.

The ceremony was held in Musgrave Park Hospital, a familiar place to me in my early years when I was fitted with artificial limbs.

Among the nominated people present, was a little girl who had been horrifically burned, and a man who had been blown up by a landmine. He had lost both of his legs and one arm. There were small children with tremendous courage who had terminal illness who were being recognised for their bravery. It was a very humbling experience, and I felt a bit guilty to be receiving an award along with so many brave young people.

I met an old school friend of mine who had her young daughter with her. Her little girl had been nominated the previous year also, and was battling with a brain tumour. She had recently been told by a specialist that she was going blind. The little girl was the same age as Russell, and I couldn't contain my grief, she was such a beautiful young girl, and she knew what was going to happen to her. The tears ran down my cheeks and my throat dried up. The little girl and her Mother were so brave! My award lay in the cupboard until recently, as I felt so unworthy compared to the others who received them.

Now it hangs proudly in my living room, I have contented myself that someone was thoughtful enough to give me the award and I am grateful that I was considered worthy.

CHAPTER NINETEEN

Will Guinness carry the can?

I still had the business of my claim for back payment to deal with. I left the form undone, but I had to deal with it. I was borrowing money for expenses from everywhere, my phone bill was enormous! Most of my trips to and from London were funded out of Eddie's redundancy money, and it had dried up long ago. Neither Eddie nor myself had much experience of the DHSS claim procedure, so we went together to our local social security office to ask for advice. The guy was extremely helpful and we were told we would hear something soon.

We had a visit from an adjudication officer and we were 'grilled' on every aspect of our finances. As I had appealed the fact that I had been wrongly assessed when I was a single parent, I had to attend a tribunal, Eddie was in bed feeling really ill, so my nephew came with me for moral support, I felt I was going to need it! When we arrived, we were told that an agreement had been made for payment to be made to pay back every penny I had been entitled to!

However, we still had to go through with the tribunal. The girl who had come to assess my claim spoke to give the case for the DHSS, she appeared agitated, and I thought maybe she was nervous, I certainly was! Councillor Cecil Moore put my case, emphasising the fact that any trust money was not paid directly to me, but was a third party cheque for itemised goods. There were 3 independent appeal officers present, and one of them, a well-spoken middle-aged lady, spoke directly to me.

"I cannot believe what we have been reading about the treatment you have had from the DHSS. In the 10 years I have sat on this bench, I have never come across anyone who has been so unjustly treated! It is beyond belief, I am disgusted! If the DHSS hadn't come to an agreement with your councillor earlier, we were going to strongly advise you to take your case to court as you were clearly wrongly advised and your rights have been violated and neglected!"

I was impressed with the just and fair way the appeal court dealt with my case, I thought it would be futile, but I won and I was glad to have it over and done with! The adjudicator was absolutely fuming though! I hoped I would never have to cross paths with her again!

As it turned out, I only received a fraction of what I was told I was owed, £378 for 3 years and 3 months back payment! Still I decided I had had enough of battling with them, I wanted some peace and quiet!

It wasn't for long though, the appeal for the Brazilian children was proving to be futile. I was reliably informed that my original plan to take wheelchairs and other aid to the children would be a foolish venture. I was convinced by a trusted friend who knew of the lifestyle endured by children in the Brazilian countryside, that a wheelchair would simply be turned into currency by poor parents.

The thought of sending an expensive wheelchair to Brazil to be sold for a few pounds appalled me, but I had to face the facts, they were staring me in the face. I reluctantly closed the appeal and sent the money raised to a young man I had been assured would use it to help some of the children in Brazil. His name was given to me by a good contact I had made during my fact-finding for the appeal, so I am confident that at least some children will benefit, it was nowhere as much as I had hoped to do, but then some of the best intentions are never given a chance.

Beatrice and I were just sitting writing this page when I decided to phone a friend ... I think Beatrice thought someone close had died! From listening to me on the phone she knew it was dreadful news, the look on her face was one of panic, the blood has drained from mine, **THE CEASEFIRE IS OVER! THE IRA HAVE JUST BOMBED CANARY WHARF IN LONDON!**

We are sick with fear and dread! We sat stunned for ages, unable to comprehend why this has happened! Those poor frightened people in London! It is so hard to describe how we feel, we have enjoyed peace for almost 18 months, and now somehow it seems so much worse if the bombing and shooting starts again. Tonight, 9th February, 1996, will be remembered by everyone here in Northern Ireland and indeed on the mainland, possibly throughout the world as the day the IRA ended their ceasefire, and ended the happiness and hopes and dreams of every parent and child who have tasted peace and found it sweet.

In years to come, people will remember exactly what they were doing and where they were and who they were with on this night. I was with my sister laughing and joking only minutes ago, now, the look of sadness on her face will be with me forever. Like every other right thinking person in the country, we are praying for the people caught up in this horrendous outrage, and for their families and loved ones. And we are praying for peace to return again to our beautiful country, so our children will be allowed to live the way children should live.

I had been keeping in fairly regular contact over the last year with Marion, the woman who had written the heartbreaking letter to me about her baby son. I had learned more about her during our phone conversations, and we had become quite good pals. I knew she was still struggling with her case, and she had informed her MP that a member of the Thalidomide Action Group was looking into her case.

She was delighted that this new development seemed to provoke a more positive reaction than she had previously been given.

Each time we talked I felt she was becoming more and more optimistic.

In early 1995, a documentary programme was shown on TV. There was a doctor who had admitted giving lethal overdoses to mentally and physically handicapped babies. The news had been widespread earlier about his admissions, every news bulletin had reported it! Apparently he had given lethal overdoses to 2 new born babies who he judged to be suffering, and in need of a 'merciful death'.

I phoned Marion and told her to be sure to watch the documentary, as I felt it could be helpful to know that at least she was not alone with her dreadful experience. When the programme was over, I phoned the television company to tell them how glad I was that they had made the programme, I also told them that I had found it traumatic due to my own circumstances.

The guy on the other end of the phone was really helpful and gave me a contact number set up specifically to provide help and support for anyone who had a similar experience. I phoned Marion and told her about the helpline, she said she would phone straight away and would call me back later.

True to her word, she phoned shortly afterwards, the helpline listened to her and promised to send out a booklet for her to read. She was distressed but glad to know that she was not the only one who had suffered in such a way, and she felt now maybe someone would listen to her.

Before the programme had gone out, Freddie had been invited to give his opinion on the doctor's revelations to a daytime magazine programme. Freddie being meticulous as ever, found the doctor's phone number and called him. During the television interview, Freddie spoke of his earlier phone conversation with the doctor and how he had condemned the doctor's actions. The doctor obviously felt decidedly uncomfortable talking with Freddie because he was a Thalidomide victim. Freddie then finished the conversation by saying:

"Thank goodness you weren't around in the days when Thalidomide was rife, you'd have had a field day!"

The Annual Thalidomide Society meeting was due to take place in Liverpool, I felt it would be an opportunity to meet Marion in person, so I invited her to come up to meet with Freddie, Heather and myself. She agreed readily and we arranged to stay over so we could talk.

Heather and I had arranged that she would meet Marion and introduce herself as I would be arriving later. As soon as Marion spotted me she came straight over and hugged me! She had obviously recognised me from the news reports, and it was nice to finally meet her at last. We had coffee and talked for a while, and she told me her baby had been named Richard even before he was born. I was struck by the way she called him by his name every time she spoke of him.

As we had a lot of meetings to go to, Marion accompanied my niece Paula to the hotel swimming pool, and afterwards I introduced her to Freddie. As we all sat talking, she said it had meant a great deal to her to have the opportunity to meet us and talk things over.

She was a very jolly woman and seemed full of life, we all got along with her very well, and I had a lot of respect for her for not giving up on her son after what had happened. Her outlook on life was not at all what I had expected when I first read her sad, tragic letter. It is difficult for me to imagine what I would feel like if that had happened to me, Marion is obviously a survivor and I was glad we had met.

Things were happening so fast, every time I put the phone down, it would ring again! I have to admit the strain of it all was taking its toll, I didn't seem to have any time for my family let alone myself.

Eddie had remarked a few times that we hadn't spent any time alone together, but as I was so busy with commitments I really didn't take any notice. I felt I was responsible for looking after campaign business and I didn't want to let anyone down.

What I didn't realise was, I was finding it increasingly impossible to say 'NO'. Whenever anyone asked me to become involved with a project, I made the time, but everyone at home was suffering. In the space of a month 3 different woman's magazines had called to ask me to do an interview about my life as a wife and mother!

I agreed. What I didn't realise was, it takes hours upon hours to do interviews which probably only fills half a page! The photographs take forever and by the last one, Eddie and the boys were smiling grudgingly just to please me!

It had gotten to the state where even my Mum and sisters couldn't visit me, as I had the phone to my ear constantly! On one occasion, Beatrice had driven all the way to Belfast to see me, and when she arrived I was on the phone. Eddie made her a cup of tea, but she couldn't stay long. She waited and waited for me to finish on the phone, but in the end she had to go, and I hadn't even had the chance to speak to her.

However, I found it extremely easy to say 'no' when a network documentary team phoned to ask if I would be willing to take part in a programme about Thalidomide. The researcher was quite 'miffed' that I had a happy outlook and was unable to furnish her with a 'sob story'. She specifically targeted questions which I felt didn't relate to me, and because I answered in such a positive way, she let me know it was really a negative experience she was looking for.

"I'm sorry, if it's a sob story you want you've phoned the wrong person because I don't have one."

I learned later she had phoned Mum with the same request. When Mum told her she would have to speak to Dad at another address as they were divorced, she said;

"O really? Is that because your daughter was Thalidomide?"

"It had absolutely nothing to do with the way my daughter was born" Mum snapped.

One night, Eddie and I were sitting talking, we decided we both needed a break away from everything. A family holiday was needed badly! We talked well into the night, and I became acutely aware of just how much I had missed just sitting talking with Eddie. I promised him things would be a little more sedate when we came back from our holiday. Next morning, we set off for the travel agents, we waded through a mountain of brochures and decided on Cyprus … Cyprus here we come!

For the next few weeks, I spent every spare minute researching into exact details of the original Thalidomide cases. I had made quite a lot of contacts and it was becoming increasingly important that I have my facts and figures straight. The Action Group had plans for the year ahead, and we meant to make an impact but I had to read everything I could find so I would be ready if I was needed.

Eddie was still cooking and making a very good job of it too! The boys were getting used to me having the phone almost permanently glued to my ear as I kept in touch with other members of the Group. Anything I wasn't sure of, I phoned Freddie, he was a mine of information, we had to have our facts right ... we planned to attend the next Guinness shareholders meeting!

We had been given shares in Guinness PLC by a generous benefactor who wanted to help our case. We were really elated as it meant we could attend the next meeting and put our case right in front of the other shareholders. We accepted the shares with heartfelt gratitude, there were enough shares for 6 members in our group to attend. We couldn't wait! If we had the support of the other shareholders, it would mean we had crossed another bridge!

In early 1995, I received a phone call from our local radio station;

"Kim, what is your reaction to the news that Guinness have pledged £2.5 million to Thalidomide victims over the next 15 years?"

I was speechless, I really didn't have a clue what he was talking about!

"Look it up on teletext and you will be able to read the details" the reporter said.

"Can I phone you back in 5 minutes?" I asked.

I turned the television on and flipped through the teletext as fast as I could! Sure enough, Guinness had pledged £37.5 million within the next 15 years.

"Brilliant! What a great victory!" I shouted to an empty room.

I had to be careful what I said to the reporter though, because I wasn't exactly sure what the offer would mean to us. I phoned the reporter back and joked;

"Well that's me sorted out, now what about the other 457 victims?"

I explained that we were very grateful to Guinness for their kind donation, but until I had spoken with our financial expert I was unable to say what it would mean. I suggested that the money may well be conserved by the Thalidomide Trust for the next 15 years and payment from the £37.5 million would only come into effect then. This meant we would have to present our claims like charity cases just as our parents had done all those years ago! A structured settlement which we had requested, would mean the money would be payable directly to all beneficiaries. With so many of us now suffering from arthritis and other newly diagnosed problems, we needed help now. The situation was worsening, we now had less money than ever but our needs were greater! The way Guinness planned to work it, the donation would simply mean a stay of execution with no real cash benefit going directly to any of us!

Our fears were confirmed within days. The Trust planned to conserve all donations from Guinness PLC over the next 15 years! My statement to the press declared;

"The donation from Guinness meant they had given us a sticking plaster to cover a wound that needed major surgery."

I phoned the Reverend Eric Smyth to ask if he could bring the matter up in council again if possible. He said he would and wished me all the best at the Shareholders meeting as I was leaving to attend the same day.

Before the meeting began, we waited outside with a barrage of reporters, and as the shareholders arrived we handed out leaflets we had printed with our reasons for the campaign. 9 out of 10 of the shareholders simply smiled and accepted the leaflets the others walked on and completely ignored us.

Two film crews were from American television companies and we were pleased to see that news of the campaign had reached beyond the U.K. At the shareholders reception, we had to hand over our shareholders certificates. Guinness were well prepared for us, they had made provision for everyone of us to have a helper allowed access to the meeting, although company rules only allowed shareholders to attend.

After the opening minutes, we were invited to proceed to the microphones if we had any comments to make. Most members used this opportunity to address the 800 plus shareholders in attendance. Everyone spoke well and managed to get their point across, I didn't take the microphone though, as I found the tone of events going against what I felt was right.

One guy let our side down by using tactics I couldn't condone. As he talked he seemed to desperately grasp whatever pitiful comparisons he could to make his point. I saw some people wince, and I made my excuses and left the room. I put my head down and wished a hole would open up and swallow me, I couldn't go back in there! The Action Group had never before asked for anyone's pity and had never received any, we had a legitimate grievance and all we wanted was to be heard.

At the end of the meeting, I went back in to retrieve my coat, all in all, the meeting had gone well, apart from the incident, a lot of people came over and congratulated us for putting valid points across. Maybe I was a bit sensitive, but I just wanted the shareholders to realise we had a valid case.

During the meeting, Guinness made a point of referring to David Mason's comment that it was extremely generous of Guinness to have made a donation to the Thalidomide Trust Fund, particularly since they had no legal responsibility. As a parent of a Thalidomide victim, Mr Mason's opinion was very valuable.

To the Action Group, his remarks did little to help our cause, although we will be eternally grateful to Mr Mason for his vigorous and courageous fight in holding out for a better settlement all those years ago, we feel that our campaign takes on board new facts and circumstances which can only be dealt with by us, the children, of which I am one of the youngest, and I'm 33!

Outside, the reporters were waiting for our comments on how we thought the AGM had gone. We said we had received a negative response, but were determined to continue until a secure future was assured for all victims.

We were also of the opinion within our Group, that the donation from Guinness was timed to perfection, to pre-empt the shareholders meeting, and there was no doubting the huge resources and public relations of Guinness. We had come this far, and although the company was one of the biggest multi-nationals in the world, we were still determined to take them on!

It was an exhausting day, and one local reporter who I had become friendly with remarked that she would be glad to get back home as she missed her 4 children.

"You're lucky, I have another 3 days to go of meetings, I miss my kids every time I come over here!" I said.

That night, Heather and I shared a hotel room as we had to make last minute arrangements and there was only one room available. Heather had John with her and he really was a great help.

When it came time to go to bed, Heather had to be helped off with her clothes and also to do all her 'normal' bedtime routines. As I watched John prop her up in bed with lots of extra pillows (she couldn't lie flat because it was too painful), I found the ritual more than a little disturbing.

Heather was obviously very used to this, but seeing her body covered in sores and the fact that she was incontinent and unable to do even the simplest task for herself, stunned me!

I don't know what I had expected, (Heather has no legs at all just feet jutting out from the sides of her lower body, and her hands come straight out of her shoulders) after all, I have been in contact with similar disabilities all of my life, but somehow I had never fully understood what my fellow sufferers had to endure daily just to get through the day.

Unlike Heather, I have arms and legs, although they are severely shortened, but at least I can get around and do most personal things for myself. I suppose I should have felt lucky, but I didn't. I couldn't sleep at all that night, my mind was in turmoil.

The next morning, I did my best to avoid intruding on Heather while she was getting dressed. It was difficult being in the same small hotel room, but I couldn't bear to see what she had to go through again.

Later that day, we were having lunch with my MP, Peter Robinson, when I began to cry. I was so embarrassed, I made an excuse and headed straight for the ladies room. I found it difficult to keep my emotions in control, I couldn't understand what was happening to me! When I arrived home again Eddie knew immediately there was something wrong with me, but I couldn't tell him what it was ... now could I? I didn't know myself.

I think every single member of my family must have said to me over the next week or so;

"What's wrong with you Kim, you're not your usual self" or

"You've taken on far too much work, you need a break"

Whatever anyone said, I took no notice, I was drawing further and further away from everyone, and I couldn't tell any of them why, how could I expect them to understand?

I was having recurring nightmares. I woke to find myself unable to do even the simplest thing for myself! Whatever I asked my body to do, it wouldn't do it! I was totally helpless! In another nightmare, I was old and helpless, with a stranger doing everything for me, including looking after my personal hygiene, I thought I was losing my mind!

Eddie couldn't do a thing right, I complained about everything, and started rows over the silliest things. I was pushing him away. What did he want to be married to someone like me for anyway? Was he mad?

Mum, Frances, Beatrice and Joan all called to try to talk to me. Elizabeth phoned, she was worried about me too. I told everyone to just leave me, there was nothing to worry about, I was just tired. Mum insisted it must be more than just tiredness, and I told her I was having a hormone imbalance, so she made an appointment with the doctor and took me herself to make sure I went!

The arguments Eddie and I were having started to become more frequent. In my mind he couldn't win. It got to the stage where I wanted everyone to go away and leave me alone to fade away. Eddie wouldn't give in, he kept asking me what was wrong, what was upsetting me so badly? Instead of confiding in him, I pushed him to the limit of his patience with my cruel remarks.

I deliberately started a terrible row, I knew Eddie had taken almost as much as he could, I thought to myself;

"Let him go then, he's better off without me!"

After pushing him to go, he left and slammed the door behind him! It was about 1.30am, I sat staring into space. As my eyes went out of focus, I found myself looking into a deep black hole. The darkness looked comforting, and as the well of black swirled around, circling deeper and deeper down, I saw myself diving into the well and falling to the very depth where I was lost forever.

"If I just let myself tip over into it, nobody will ever have to look after me again, go on Kim, just do it!" I thought.

Suddenly I started to cry. I sobbed and sobbed as I have never done before in my life. When I had cried to the point where I could only take sharp deep bursts of breath, I lifted the phone. It rang 4 times.

"Hello ... Kim? What's wrong love? Calm down and tell me what it is" I heard Beatrice say.

For a while I just cried uncontrollably again, somehow hearing Beatrice's voice brought me back into reality again.

"Beatrice, you've got to help me, I'm being swallowed up by a big black hole and I have no power to stop it! What am I going to do?" I sobbed.

Beatrice spoke to me and calmed me down, but before she put the phone down she made sure I was totally relaxed, she said she would be up to see me as soon as she could get some clothes on and drive the 32 miles to my house. She suggested I let her phone Mum, Joan or Frances as they only live 2 miles away, but I insisted I didn't want anyone else to know! I promised her I would be okay until she arrived.

Beatrice must have driven at breakneck speed, I had only but the phone down about 20 minutes when she arrived! I was much calmer when I saw her and it was obvious I had given her a real fright! Not to mention getting her out of bed at 4 o'clock in the morning. I hadn't realised what time it was when I phoned, but when I heard the time, I realised I must have been staring into that black hole for almost three hours!

As we talked, I began to relax for the first time in a long while. I allowed myself to speak for the first time about my fears for the future, and how seeing Heather had really affected me. Just talking about it helped a lot, and when Russell got up for school at 7 o'clock, I had composed myself and was feeling much better.

My main concern once I had calmed down, was for Eddie, where had he gone? What would he do? I had really pushed him! What if he had done something in a moment of madness? My mind was racing. Beatrice started to phone around to leave messages for Eddie to contact home.

That afternoon, Eddie arrived home and we talked for a long time. I had hurt Eddie by shutting him out and not allowing him to help me when I was feeling so bad. It had never occurred to me how he must have felt while he watched his wife fall deeper and deeper into a depressed state, it must have been horrible!

I phoned Beatrice later and thanked her for being there for me when I needed her. But I made her promise not to tell Mum or anyone else what had happened. I still felt a little raw, and I needed time to sort things out in my head. Now with Eddie to help me, I could work through how I felt with him, as I now knew I should have done in the first place ... keeping it to myself had almost been the end of me!

CHAPTER TWENTY

Our children ... innocent heirs?

On my return from London, I had received a phone call from Reverend Eric Smith. He said his name had been put forward for the position of Lord Mayor of Belfast! It was the first I had heard and I wished him all the best. If anyone deserved it, he did!

As he continued, he said he wondered if I would consider being the guest speaker at the Lord Mayor's Initiation Dinner, assuming he was successful of course. I was deeply honoured to be asked, and more than a little overwhelmed at the prospect of making a speech in front of so many people at such a prestigious event!

I was feeling much more like my old self again after my 'dark days', so I was glad of the opportunity to get into the swing of things again, although I wanted to take things a little more relaxed, as I'm sure the pressure of so many commitments hadn't helped me. I wished Eric the best of luck and looked forward to the results of the Mayor's election.

A few days later, I watched the television with added enthusiasm, to see the result of the council vote, I was overjoyed to watch as Eric emerged in his back and gold robes, the new Lord Mayor of Belfast!

A month before the 'big day', I was sitting discussing arrangements for the Ball, having been invited to the City Hall by Eric. The organiser was going over the details of what the night's events would entail. Eric declared:

"Kim and I won't be needing any speeches, what we have to say will come from the heart."

I sat with my mouth open, frozen to the spot, no speech .... AAA-R-GH!

Arrangements had to be made to accommodate my wheelchair. I went to City Hall again and Eric came up with an ingenious plan to have a platform made specially for me. I would sit in a normal chair, and the Master of Ceremonies and Eddie would discreetly lift me onto the platform when the time came for me to deliver my speech. We were confident the plan would work!

One of the officials could see I was a little apprehensive about my speech.

"Kim, if you would like, I can have your speech printed out for you, just put down what you want to say, and I'll have it printed out ready to read," he offered.

It sounded like a good idea to me, so I accepted. I was going to need all the help I could get!

I practised and practised, and when the day arrived I was a total wreck! My stomach felt as if there was a convention of neurotic butterflies going on in the basement! I went to the hairdressers and had my hair put up in an elegant french pleat. The hairdresser was pleased with the result, and it was lovely, so I paid the man and got out of there fast!

When I arrived home, I got straight into a shower and washed my hair, all those ringlets and quiffs just didn't feel like me and I was nervous enough without looking and feeling like a barbie doll!

When the time arrived to set off for City Hall, a stretch limousine pulled up outside my house! Eddie had ordered it as a treat. I felt like Royalty! We drove over to Mum's house and picked her and Alex up. Eric had kindly included tickets for two guests.

Before the ceremony I was called to the Lord Mayor's parlour to have photographs taken. While we were there I handed my precious speech to Mum to hold for me. When we were making our way back to the social room, I asked Mum to give me my speech back. She handed me a booklet with all the guests names on it. I opened it up ... NO SPEECH! It had gone!

My stomach turned over and started to do somersaults, the butterfly convention had moved out, the chinese flying acrobats were giving the performance of their lives! I felt the colour drain from my face. Eric must have noticed I was looking a little green around the gills as he came over and asked me what was wrong.

"I've lost my speech! what will I do?" I said.

"It must be there, it was there a minute ago!" Mum said desperately trying to calm me down.

"We'll find it, don't worry" he soothed.

The other guess all left and went into the Grand Hall. As it turned out someone had found my speech and was just about to hand it to the Master of Ceremonies when Alex, who was frantic at the time, walked straight over and grabbed it from him.

"Thank you!" he said more out of relief than rudeness.

About half way through the ceremony, Eddie and the Toast Master lifted me onto the platform as arranged, ready to give my speech. The time was drawing near, there was no backing out, I was terrified. A sheer bolt of confidence hit me!

"My Lord Lieutenant, Minister, Deputy Lord Mayor, High Sheriff, Reverend Sirs, Your Worships, My Lord Aldermen, Councillors, Ladies and Gentlemen ... I give you a toast, Eric Smyth, Lord Mayor of Belfast!"

Phew! I was glad to get that mouthful over and done with. I spoke for twenty minutes but honestly can't remember making the speech, but I'm told I sailed through it without making a single mishap! Mum was so nervous she can hardly remember, I think losing my speech traumatised her for the rest of the night!

I was told by a City Official that he had initially been opposed to having me as a guest speaker, as usually someone of high office or a senior official was selected to speak at official ceremonies. He congratulated me and said they had received so many compliments from the guests. He was very pleased that Eric's choice had proved so popular and successful.

One guest had told him that my speech had made such an impact on him that he would never forget me. Eric added his enthusiastic congratulations and told me he had met with a lot of opposition because of his choice of speaker, but he was adamant and stood by his decision, as he had every faith in me! Thank goodness I didn't know that from the start or I would never have had the nerve to do it!

In July we set off for Cyprus, happy days! My sister Frances and her husband and two children were going with us. I was really looking forward to speaking time with Eddie and the boys.

We had been to Cyprus before, but not with the boys as they usually went to visit their Dad in the summer. I really wanted them to be with me for a while as we had so much time to make up for. The people were so friendly and the whole holiday was just so relaxing!

I realised how tense and uptight I had been once I actually had the first couple of days over me! I had a go at paragliding - it was brilliant! I couldn't get enough of it! I had wanted to do it for a long time, but had never had the opportunity.

We met up with Michelle and David, a Scottish couple we had befriended on a previous holiday to Cyprus. We had a whale of a time together as the boys had never been abroad before, so everything was fascinating for them.

Russell and I had a go on a jet-ski. I had Russell standing in front of me to hold the controls, we must have been going at tremendous speed as we rushed into wave after wave, it was so exhilarating and great fun! When we finished, I was black and blue all over as Russell had been bumping into my chest and arms every time we went over a wave! I wouldn't have missed it for anything though!

The best thing was the peace and quiet, no phone ringing, no visitors, no letters, no Action Group .... heaven! It was such a relief to my system to let my hair down and enjoy myself unreservedly, I have to say it was the best holiday I've ever had, I really needed it!

Before long I was back to reality with a bump! I was down at City Hall to help with arrangements for the Lord Mayor's charity for spina bifida and hydrocephalus. I had offered to do a parachute jump in aid of charity and was making plans.

I heard a familiar voice;

"Kim, can I have a word with you?" Eric said.

My first reaction was, "What have I done now!"

He brought me into his office and asked me if I had ever considered writing a book about myself. I think he was a bit taken aback when I told him that Beatrice and I had been talking about writing a book for nearly 20 years!

We had often talked about our childhood and laughed together and promised each other we would write a book someday! Over the years we had written little snippets after family get-togethers for 'our book'. Recently we had made an effort to gather more information, but as often happens, events took over in both our lives and we had put it off yet again.

"Why do you ask?" I enquired.

"I've been asked by a publisher to ask you if you would be interested in writing a book. Would you mind if I passed your phone number on?" He asked me.

"No, I don't mind at all," I answered.

When I finally reached home, I phoned Beatrice and told her the news. There was no way I would even consider writing a book without her, after all, it was something we had been planning to do together for years! She didn't believe me at first, but once I had convinced her I was serious she began to read all the little snippets she had been collecting out loud to me over the phone.

She is the one in our family we would always ask if there was something in our childhood we couldn't remember, as she has a great memory for detail from way back (and besides that she can type!). We started writing immediately after a meeting with the publishers.

In November 1995, Heather, Freddie, Glenn (another of our group) and myself headed off to London to meet with the Chairman of Guinness. He had finally agreed to meet with us and we were hopeful but apprehensive. It was an important meeting and we were looking forward to hearing what he had to say about our campaign.

Mum travelled with me this time, and it was a treat for me to be able to spend so much time alone with her. When you're the youngest of seven, getting your Mother all to yourself is like a military operation I can tell you!

The meeting with the Chairman was disappointing. We were informed that as far as Guinness were concerned they had donated £37.5 million to be paid over the next 15 years to the trust fund and that was all they were prepared to discuss. He went on to say that different avenues had been looked into and it had been decided that a structured settlement would not be in our best interests! He then said that they had appointed an expert to research into the best way to invest the £37.5 million.

Freddie could contain himself no longer.

"Whoever your researcher was must have had one Guinness to many!" He said.

We all burst out laughing right there on the spot when he came off with that one! We went with our barrister and financial advisor and consoled ourselves. Our barrister, Jacqueline Perry said she would continue to act for us no matter what. I knew she wouldn't let us down and we were delighted as she is considered amongst the top barristers in Britain. As we talked, I could see that my Mum was unusually quiet. When it was time to leave, Mum could hardly speak but was determined to say something to Jacqueline and Anthony Scrivener, QC and Stephen Ashcroft, our financial expert who had all worked tirelessly as our legal team. With her voice full of emotion and tears in her eyes she said,

"Do you mind if I say something? If the parents had been represented by a legal team of people as devoted and caring as you .... the Thalidomide Action Group would never have needed to be here today!"

When Mum finished, she began to cry, she was so embarrassed. I made a joke to try to relax her, as I knew deep down the whole episode had brought back bad memories of the years of wrangling our parents had gone through.

"Well, that's the last time I bring you anywhere with me! I can't bring her anywhere but she has to start crying and embarrassing me! If you keep that up, you won't be coming with me again!" I joked with her.

Heather, Freddie and Glenn were good sports and Mum soon calmed down. We had a very friendly afternoon together despite the negative result we had received from Guinness.

While talking to Glenn, I asked him how his little girl was doing. She was only two years old. Recently, we had learned that there were at least nine babies who were born to Thalidomide victims with similar deformities, to the Thalidomide parent, including my own son, Marc.

Hearing about the other babies made me thankful that Marc only had an extra thumb, which was rectified by surgery. Others were much worse. As we gathered more information there appeared to be striking common denominators in each child's circumstance.

In most instances the baby who had been born deformed was the opposite sex to the Thalidomide parent. They were also likely to be a third child! Although we have no solid proof, and indeed the medical 'experts' dispute any possibility of a genetic link, the fact is that the incidence of deformity in our children is very high, not to mention their deformities are practically identical!

A doctor in Sydney, called McBride, who by the way was one of the first to alert the world to the Thalidomide babies in the late 50's, wrote in the British Medical Journal and held a conference in Dublin recently where he talked of his belief that there was indeed evidence that genetic damage was a distinct possibility with Thalidomide.

Our group believe that there may well be more second generation babies who have been born with their parent's legacy of deformity. However, I was unaware until recently that there were other children besides Marc. In Glenn's case, his daughter had to have both of her feet amputated just like her Dad. Her hands are strikingly similar to her Dad's although she has two fingers on each hand whereas Glenn has only one.

Another doctor, who sits on the panel representing Guinness, who assesses new claimants for Thalidomide trust status, stated in a Medical Journal that the incidence of deformed children being born to Thalidomide victims was merely coincidence.

Any parent will understand the heartbreaking implications, if indeed the legacy of Thalidomide is passed on to our children or our grandchildren. If anyone knows exactly what life is like being severely deformed, we do. For a drug to have caused such devastating deformities in thousands of babies is scandalous to say the least, but if those same deformities are being passed on to subsequent generations through genetic damage, then we should know the truth.

Those of us who have voiced our fears about second generation babies, including Glenn and myself, have been told that if we persist in our claim we will be taken off the list of 'official Thalidomide victims' currently in receipt of funds, and will receive no further payments. When we asked how they could explain the fact that we have been officially Thalidomide most of our lives, we we told that it could simply be explained away by stating we had 'slipped through the net' and were not Thalidomide at all! I can't help thinking I've heard that threat somewhere before.

We're not seeking compensation for our children who have tragically been the innocent heirs to our deformities, it was nigh impossible first time around. But it is of primary importance to us to know if there is a genetic link. There are numerous tests for other genetic conditions whereby parents can be told if their baby will be born with a defect, surely it is perfectly natural for us to want to know also?

Our children are our future, and the innocence of children and their ideas about the world around them is wonderful! I was asked recently to give a talk to some local children who were planning to visit a disabled centre. The organisers of the community centre thought it would be a good idea if the boys and girls had the chance to meet a disabled person, and have their questions answered about the problems associated with being disabled, before their visit.

I had a thoroughly enjoyable day with the children as I talked about my childhood and how I was the youngest of seven children. I told the children that I still had to do my share of the housework, mainly the floor level jobs like washing dirty skirting boards and cleaning the fridge out. They laughed and seemed to enjoy some of my stories.

At the end of my talk, I invited the children to ask me questions. The boys and girls were very interested and asked a variety of questions which I answered as well as I could. However, one little girl about nine years old asked me a question I had never thought about before:

"Why do you think God made you like you are, instead of one of your brothers or sisters?"

I was surprised by her question, but without having to think about it I said;

"Well my oldest brother, Alex, is a captain in the army and is in charge of physical training. Frances (who worked for the community centre) drives a bus; Trevor loves football and could have been a professional if he'd been given the chance when he was younger; Beatrice teaches aerobics; Elizabeth is a hairdresser and spends most of her day on her feet and Joan loves gymnastics. Every one of them enjoy doing things which would be very difficult to do if they were disabled, so I think I was the only one who never really wanted to do things like that, because all I ever wanted to do was sing .... and you can do that sitting down!"

Thalidomide - the facts

Thalidomide was first made available in Britain in April 1958, the brand name was Distaval. During the three and a half years it was in distribution, the Ministry of Health made an initial conservative estimate claiming 250 babies had survived. In actual fact the real figure was nearer to 450. No figures are available for the children who died at birth or were killed or may even be alive but undiscovered even today.

The distributors, DISTILLERS, had reports of numerous cases of severe nerve damage (peripheral neuritis) to hundreds of Thalidomide users, and did consider withdrawing the drug, but because of an unusual contract of marketing the drug, they continued distribution. This decision was to have tragic consequences in the form of hundreds of babies being born with horrible deformities, why was this allowed to happen?

A catalogue of oversights coupled with the then inadequate rules regulating the distribution of any new drug combined to cause what became known as 'The Thalidomide Scandal'.

Distillers accepted the drug based on incomplete tests carried out by the German company who made the drug, 'Chemie Gruenenthal'. Distillers did not take enough care to discover research which provided written evidence that Thalidomide could cause 'monster births'.

They ignored the fact that Thalidomide could damage the nervous system, even though scientific research at the time showed this to be a warning of possible foetal damage. Even then, the advertisements claimed that the drug was perfectly safe for pregnant women.

There were no animal tests done to determine if foetal damage could occur. In fact the commercial advertising was given top priority to speed up sales as the drug was claimed to be a wonder drug.

The tragedy could have been avoided, had thorough tests been carried out and early warning signs been taken into account. Some testing was eventually ordered to be carried out by 5 specialists, but as the Distillers firm wanted to begin marketing in January, final results would take longer.

One doctor, Dr Thiersch, injected pregnant rats with aminopterin and found that the foetuses were actually absorbed into the mother's flesh or died in the womb. Thalidomide would be useful in inducing abortions, he suggested. Twelve women were involved in the experiment. Ten of them had their babies die in the womb, and aborted, the other 2 had to have surgical abortions. His report showed 3 foetuses were obviously seriously deformed.

AMINOPTERIN is a chemical closely related to Thalidomide, it is a member of the TERATOGENIC family of drugs known to cause 'monster births' as early as 1950. Dr Thiersch's study was not picked up by Distillers.

In November 1958, an intensive advertising campaign was structured by Distillers. The main theme was to be absolute safety. One poster showed a little child reaching up to a shelf containing a bottle of Distaval with the words 'non-toxic, completely safe'.

Another report made available to Distillers, claimed that the thyroid was affected by Thalidomide, and advised that until more detailed research was completed the drug should not be marketed.

Distillers, however, had a deadline to meet to conform to their contract with the German company and went ahead with the marketing. The drug Thalidomide was recommended for neurology, dermatology, dentistry, obstetrics and paediatrics. The appeal of the drug was that it was completely safe and at the time there were regular media reports of deaths due to barbituate overdose or poisoning. Thalidomide looked like the perfect answer to a mounting problem.

A pharmacologist working for Distillers, found that the drug was highly toxic in some forms, particularly liquid. The same doctor began to look at the effects Thalidomide had on the nervous system prompted by other reports from a doctor treating a patient with possible p. neuritis.

Chemie Gruenenthal were now receiving reports of Thalidomide being linked with p. neuritis, epilepsy, speech loss, and rashes, the drug was not only unsafe, it was dangerous and appeared to be the cause of some serious conditions. Distillers went ahead and marketed the liquid form of Thalidomide.

The liquid version was described in marketing 'specially flavoured to suit all palates' and 'particularly suited for administration to children'. Although reports were starting to come in regularly about illnesses due to Thalidomide, Distillers answer was to try to educate the doctors prescribing the drug to watch their patients for any signs of trouble whilst using the drug.

The British Medical Journal carried an advertisement of assurance stating that 'There is no case on record in which even a gross overdose with Distaval has had harmful results. Put your mind at rest. Depend on the safety of Distaval.' The same issue that month, carried 3 letter relating to cases of p. neuritis.

Meanwhile babies were being born with 'monster-like' deformities in various parts of Britain. It was early 1961.

In Australia, a Doctor McBride had done research work with Thalidomide using the New Zealand white rabbit. Doctor McBride voiced his concerns to the Distillers sales representative, and was disturbed to hear from the sales rep. that his own child had been born disabled after his wife had taken Distaval. A report outlining Doctor McBride's fears was passed on to the Distillers directors. The report, Distillers claimed, was never received. It was the Queen's official birthday, June 1961.

His report showed definite proof of foetal deformity. He reported that Distaval would not go down in history as the wonder drug it was hailed as, but would be most likely responsible for a terrible tragedy. Five months later, having heard nothing from Distillers in response to his earlier warnings, he sent further reports. Two days later trials on rats began to test McBride's theory. Chemie Gruenenthal were informed, and it came to light that a Professor in Hamburg had found 14 mothers of deformed babies who had without doubt used the drug Distaval. The tests began on 23rd November, 1961.

Still the drug was not withdrawn. A report next day in a German paper prompted a meeting of the company's directors where they decided to stop distribution of Distaval. News was passed on to Distillers who after overwhelming proof decided to take the drug off the market also.

Not so with hospital sales though. They instructed their sales reps to step up promotion of the drug to hospitals. Despite promotional advertising in the LANCET, sales continued to fall prompting the company to discontinue sales to hospitals as well. It was December, 1962.

In August 1962, the year before his assassination, President JF Kennedy presented Frances O Kelsey with the President's award for Distinguished Federal Civilian Service. Dr Kelsey had saved many American babies from the horror of Thalidomide by preventing the drug from being distributed in America. Her job as physician with the Food and Drugs Administration, authorised her to prevent a drug being licensed if she believed it was dangerous. Frances O Kelsey believed the drug could cause deformities in unborn babies. She was right. As far as we know the last such baby to be born in the U.K. was in June 1962, her name was Kim.